Battlefield
of the
FOR
TEENS mind

JOYCE MEYER

WITH TODD HAFER

Battlefield
of the
mind

FOR
TEENS

WINNING THE BATTLE
IN YOUR MIND

Faith
Words

NEW YORK BOSTON NASHVILLE

Unless otherwise indicated, all Scripture quotations are taken from the *Holy Bible, New International Version*®. NIV®. Copyright © 1973, 1978, 1984 by International Bible Society. Used by permission of Zondervan Publishing House. All rights reserved.

Scripture quotations marked NASB are taken from the *New American Standard Bible*. Copyright © The Lockman Foundation 1960, 1962, 1963, 1968, 1971, 1972, 1973, 1975, 1977, 1995. Used by permission.

Scripture quotations marked TLB are taken from *The Living Bible* © 1971. Used by permission of Tyndale House Publishers, Inc., Wheaton, Illinois 60189.

Scripture quotations marked NKJV are taken from *The New King James Version*. Copyright © 1979, 1980, 1982, Thomas Nelson, Inc.

Scripture quotations marked KJV are taken from the *King James Version* of the Bible.

Scripture quotations marked AMP are taken from *The Amplified Bible*. *Old Testament* copyright © 1965, 1987 by Zondervan Corporation, Grand Rapids, Michigan. *New Testament* copyright © 1958, 1987 by The Lockman Foundation, La Habra, California. Used by permission.

FaithWords
Hachette Book Group
1290 Avenue of the Americas, New York, NY 10104
www.faithwords.com.

Printed in the United States of America

First Edition: June 2006
22

FaithWords is a division of Hachette Book Group, Inc.
The FaithWords name and logo is a trademark of Hachette Book Group, Inc.

Library of Congress Cataloging-in-Publication Data

Meyer, Joyce
Battlefield of the mind for teens : winning the battle in your mind /
Joyce Meyer with Todd Hafer.—1st ed.
p. cm.
Summary: "A guide to overcoming the worries of the world, written
specifically for teen readers"—Provided by the publisher.
Includes bibliographical references.
ISBN 978-0-446-69764-4
1. Christian teenagers—Religious life. 2. Thought and thinking—Religious aspects—
Christianity. 3. Spiritual warfare. I. Hafer, Todd. II. Title.
BV4531.3.M49 2006

248.8'3—dc22   2005034011

CONTENTS

PART ONE

It's All About
the Mind

INTRODUCTION

I magine this: You're watching your favorite TV show and, right in the middle of the most exciting part, a news anchorwoman cuts in. "We interrupt this program to bring you a special news bulletin," she says. "The entire populations of Montana, South Dakota, Wyoming, Alaska, Vermont, and North Dakota have become stricken by a sexually transmitted disease! Stay tuned to this station for more details. And have a pleasant evening—unless you happen to live in Montana, South Dakota, Wyoming, Alaska, Vermont, or North Dakota!"

How would you respond to this news? Would you be shocked? Skeptical? Worried? Well, believe it or not, the scenario above isn't completely imaginary. Every year, more than four million teens—that's the equivalent of the population of all those states I just mentioned—contract a sexually transmitted disease. That's right, teens, just like you.

Teens face other problems, as well. The challenges you face as teens today aren't just sexual. By the time they graduate from high school, 56 percent of teens are regular drinkers, and 40 percent will be binge-drinkers. Today, eight teens will die as a result of alcohol. Tomorrow will be the same sad story. And the next day, and the next. . . . Alcohol is a key factor in the three leading causes of teen death: auto accident, homicide, and suicide.

Do you hear heartbreaking facts like these and wonder *Why?* I have asked the same question. Fortunately, God's Word has the answers. You might think that peer pressure, the media, or poor parenting and adult leadership are to blame. And you might be right, at least partially. But the most crucial battle you will fight in your efforts to live a meaningful, safe, satisfying life won't be fought in the halls of your school, at an after-prom party, in Internet chat sessions, or even in front of the television. The most epic fight of them all will be fought in the battlefield of your mind. I want to help make sure that the good guys win.

Proverbs 23:7 tells us, "For as [a person] thinks in his heart, so is he" (NKJV). In other words, your attitude determines your actions. Think of your body as a state-of-the-art computer; your mind is the hard drive. It runs everything else. If your hard drive gets corrupted—or crashes—it doesn't matter how high-def your monitor is, how loud your speakers are, or how fast your Internet connection is. If the hard drive is compromised, your computer is, at best, a giant paperweight, a monument to lost potential and wasted money.

I have been helping people like you better understand God's Word for almost thirty years, and the longer I serve Him and study His Word, the more I realize how important thoughts and words are. I truly believe that God's Holy Spirit has been leading me to study the Battle for the Mind and give a report directly from the frontlines to you.

I want you to win the battle for *your* mind. I want you to win big. And I want you to be able to help others win, too.

Your first step toward victory is truly understanding Proverbs 23:7—the verse that promises us that how we think of ourselves determines who we are. One Bible translation adds a key insight. It says, "As a man thinks in his heart, so does he become." Did you catch the subtle difference between the two translations? That's right, the battle for your mind not only decides who you are as a person right now—but also who you will be in the future.

Your life, your actions, will always be a direct result of your thoughts. If you have a negative mind-set, you will have a negative life. But if you renew your mind according to God's plan for you, you will have an abundant life. It's that simple.

Your life might be very difficult right now. Ninety-nine percent of high-school students say they suffer from stress at least some of the time. But don't give up. Don't despair or become cynical. Little by little, you can change. The fact that you are reading these words right now shows that you have at least some hope.

Keep hoping. Keep striving to change your mind for the better. Because when you change your mind for the better, you change your life for the better. When you begin to see God's amazing plan for your life, you'll want to follow it.

I pray that this book will help you win the battle for your mind—and the battle for your life.

This Is Your Mind . . .
This Is Your Mind
in a Battle

For our struggle is not against flesh and blood,
but against the rulers, against the authorities,
against the powers of this dark world and against
the spiritual forces of evil in the heavenly realms.
—Ephesians 6:12

A re you feeling a little tired lately? Confused? Depressed? Kicked-around? It's no wonder—you're in a war.

However, your war isn't a conventional battle that can be fought with conventional weapons. Take a look at the scripture that begins this chapter. This warfare isn't with other human beings. Not your arch nemesis at school. Not your teachers. Not your ex-boyfriend or girlfriend. Not even your parents.

Your enemy is Satan himself, the ex-angel-turned-devil—and

his demonic forces. (The Amplified version of the Bible calls them "master spirits.") Satan's coming after you with a carefully crafted plan of attack, one you might not even see coming. In fact, you might not even believe you're in a war at all. That's one of your enemy's best tricks—deception.

Satan is a liar. Jesus called him "the father of lies and of all that is false" (John 8:44 AMP). Here are some of his deceptive lines, which he'll use as he tries to control your mind. How many of them have you heard, in one form or another?

- You don't need to listen to your parents, your pastor, your youth leaders, and all those other people who try to tell you how to live. I mean, look at 'em, those incompetent hypocrites. Look at all their flaws and inconsistencies. This is *your* life. Live it your way.
- Drinking, drugs, and sex won't really hurt you. All of those horror stories won't happen to you. It's just a big scare tactic. Adults just don't want you to have any fun—even though they had plenty when they were your age. They just want to control you.
- Do you really believe in "the devil"? Some red-skinned bald dude with a pointy tail and a pitchfork? An intelligent person like you? Get real—that's a myth. There is no devil, and there is no hell. And, by the way, there is no God or heaven, either. "Right now" is all there is. So, get yours while you can.
- Come on, admit it: You have doubts about God all the time. If God was real, why would He allow those doubts to creep up inside of your head?
- If there really was a God who cared, would you feel as lonely as you do, as overwhelmed by life as you do, as powerless to change things?

Have you ever felt like someone was peppering your mind with questions and concerns like these? That's how Satan works. He plants all kinds of nagging thoughts, suspicions, and doubts in your mind. He moves slowly, according to his well-laid plans for you. Always remember that when it comes to destroying your life, Satan has a custom-tailored battle strategy just for you. He has studied you for a long time. And he's going to attack you where you're weak, where you're curious, where you're inconsistent.

For example, he knows your insecurities. If you are self-conscious about your physical appearance, the devil might devise a plan to bring someone into your life who tells you that you're hot, someone who makes you feel attractive. Then, this person you've welcomed into your life might start to pressure you for sex. You know you shouldn't, but you don't want to risk losing someone who makes you feel so good about yourself.

So now Satan can sit back and watch you squirm. He's put his secret weapon in place. He has time—and your raging hormones— on his side. He knows that you can't click on the TV, power up your computer, or open a magazine without seeing sexual content of some sort. (For example, there are more than 4 million pornographic Web sites on the Internet.) He'll invest as much time as it takes to bring you down. The devil is short in a lot of areas, but patience isn't one of them. He has patience to spare.

Fortunately for you, you're not going into the battle unarmed. The Bible, God's holy message, assures you, "For the weapons of our warfare are not physical [weapons of flesh and blood], but they are mighty before God for the overthrow and destruction of strongholds, [Inasmuch as we] refute arguments and theories and reasonings and every proud and lofty thing that sets itself up against the [true] knowledge of God; and we lead every thought and purpose away captive into the obedience of Christ (the Messiah, the Anointed one)" (2 Corinthians 10:4-5 AMP).

Now, you might be asking yourself, *What are these "strongholds" that I'm supposed to overthrow and destroy?* Think of it this way: Satan wants to play you like a video game, conquering one level at a time. Let's go back to our sexual-temptation example. Satan's not going to try to turn you from a pure person into a promiscuous, out-of-control sex addict overnight.

No, he's much more likely to get you interested in a sexually suggestive-yet-mainstream movie—the kind that's in movie theaters and on basic cable TV all the time. Or maybe an Internet chat room where the conversation occasionally—but not all the time—turns inappropriate.

Next, you might find yourself visiting Web sites you know you shouldn't, or taking your interest in suggestive movies to the next level—graduating from typical cable fare to pay-per-view stuff that turns up the sexual heat.

And so it goes. The same kind of thing happens with drugs, drinking, cheating, and lying. How many of your friends have you heard lying to their parents, via cell phone, about where they are, whom they are with, and what they are doing? Those lies, most likely, were probably more innocuous at first—like "Sure, Mom, I ate breakfast this morning," or, "Honest, Dad, we weren't assigned any homework this weekend." But those "Level 1" lies soon became Level 2, and so on.

Are you beginning to see Satan's sneaky war strategy? Is it scaring you, at least a little? Good. Every good soldier approaches battle with a heightened sense of awareness. Only a fool would charge into a war and not be aware of what is at stake.

The Dirty Dozen: 12 Ways Today's Teens Are Losing the Battle for Their Minds—and for Their Lives

1. Almost half of all 9th- through 12th-graders have had sex—including 61 percent of high-school seniors. (And teens who watch lots of sex on TV are more than twice as likely to have sex as those who are more discerning about their TV viewing.)[1,2]

2. Nearly half of people under the age of 21 who drink alcohol, binge-drink. (Binge-drinking is defined as having five or more drinks on one occasion.) More than 500,000 young people are unintentionally injured every year while under the influence of alcohol. And about 1,500 of this number die as a direct result of alcohol abuse, such as alcohol poisoning.[3]

3. Seventy-three percent of teens say they see at least one act of discrimination a month, but only 22 percent speak up and do something about it.[4]

4. Parents and teens are not on the same page—or even in the same book—when it comes to sex. While half of today's teens are sexually active, 84 percent of parents believe their kids are *not* sexually active. Meanwhile, 87 percent of teens say it would be easier to delay sex if they could have more open, honest talks with parents.[5]

5. One in six of today's young females are drunk when they lose their virginity. (One in seven say their partner was drunk, as well.)[6]

6. The United States has the highest STD and teen-pregnancy rates in the developed world. In fact, the U.S. rate of teen pregnancy is double that of any other industrialized nation.[7]

7. Suicide is the third leading cause of death among Americans ages 15 to 24.[8]

8. More than 4 million teens become infected with an STD each year.[9]

9. Almost one in four 8th-graders has tried "huffing"—using household chemicals like paint thinner or type corrector to get high.[10]

10. Every year in the United States, more than 800,000 girls 19 and under get pregnant.[11]

11. The average age at which teens start taking drugs is 13.[12]

12. Among sexually active high-school seniors, more than 21 percent have had four or more sex partners.[13]

Okay, let's take a look at what we've learned so far.

1. You are engaged in a war.

2. Satan is your enemy.

3. Your own mind is the battleground.

4. The devil will work diligently to establish strongholds in your mind, conquering the territory piece by piece, just like a master gamer conquers a video game.

5. The devil works to achieve victory by strategy and deceit—battle plans and lies. One of his best lies is to convince you that he doesn't exist.

6. Your enemy is in no hurry. He's going to take his time. He doesn't need to win now. He just wants to win in the end.

Now, let's move on to the next chapter and see another way that a satanic plan can work its cruel results.

CHAPTER 2

John, Mary, and the Blended Family That Doesn't Wanna Blend

Every family has its problems, but a teen named Mary and her stepfather feel like their family suffers from more drama and trauma than any show on UPN. Here are their two sides of the same sad story.

Mary's Got a Problem: "My stepdad is totally ruining my life!"

Mary's biological mom divorced Mary's bio-dad and remarried a man named John two years later. Seventeen-year-old Mary and her new dad are at war almost all the time. She resents him because his presence killed all hopes of Mary's mom and "real dad" getting back together.

She's so angry all the time that she cannot concentrate in school, and her stomach gets upset every time she tries to eat. Her solution: Don't eat, unless she feels like she's going to pass out.

Mary doesn't want John to run her life. She resents his curfews, his time limits on the computer and phone, and his strict punishments. He even tries to influence how she spends her money, which she earns by doing household chores. She wants him to "back off!"—which she screams at him an average of 5.8 times daily.

At this point, some of you might be thinking, *Whoa, Mary really needs to turn her life over to Jesus!*

The problem is she did that—when she was twelve. She was sincere about her decision. She believes she's going to heaven, and her anger toward her stepdad makes her feel guilty and sad. She does see hope for her life, but that hope seems a long way off. "Before I met Jesus," she tells a friend in her youth group, "I was hopeless and miserable; now, I'm just miserable."

Mary knows her attitude is wrong. She wants to change. She has spent hours in counseling with her youth pastor and has even gone to the counselor at school. She prays about her struggle every night. She is bewildered about why she hasn't seen any lasting improvement in the situation. "Why isn't this getting better?"

she sobs to herself one night. "I'm so tired of being miserable all the time."

The solution to Mary's problem can be found in Romans 12:2: "Do not conform any longer to the pattern of this world, but be transformed by the renewing of your mind. Then you will be able to test and approve what God's will is—his good, pleasing and perfect will."

You see, Mary's mind is littered with strongholds. Some have been there since she first heard the word *divorce* uttered in her house. She knows she shouldn't harbor the bitter, resentful thoughts about her stepfather, but she can't seem to purge them from her head.

Mary can't control her tantrums, her blatant disregard for "house rules," and her hateful words, because she can't control the thoughts behind them. She can't remove the strongholds that the devil has planted in her mind.

Satan has constructed effective lies. All through the divorce proceedings, Mary became angrier and angrier at the situation. But she didn't want to direct her anger at her biological parents because she adored them both. She didn't want to think that two people she respected so much could be responsible for a situation that was tearing her insides apart.

And that's when Satan's lies started: "You, Mary, are the reason behind the divorce. They fight because of you. You cost them a lot of money. They worry about your grades. You make them stressed out, and that's why they fight."

And there were other lies, too: "I bet that your parents have fallen out of love. Your mom wishes she had married someone else. Your dad feels the same way. I bet there is infidelity involved here."

As a result, Mary resolved a couple of things in her mind:

1. "If my behavior broke up one marriage, it can do it again. If I can make John totally miserable, maybe he'll leave and my real mom and dad can be together again."
2. "I bet John was hitting on my mom back when she was still married to Dad. He's slimy. He should have just left us alone. Now, I'm gonna make him pay! He'll wish he never came near my family!"

Imagine all the lies playing in Mary's head, month after month, on a continuous loop. Lies that deepen Mary's resentment toward John and her obsession with breaking up a marriage. Is it any wonder she's not the sweet, adoring daughter she once was? How can Mary pull herself out of her misery? What would you do if you were in her place?

Unleash Your Weapons

If you abide in My word [hold fast to My teachings and live
in accordance with them], you are truly My disciples.
And you will know the Truth, and the Truth will set you free.
—John 8:31-32 AMP

In this verse, Jesus tells us how we can go upside Satan's head and break free of his grip when he attacks us: We must absorb the knowledge of God's truth into our minds and hearts, renewing our minds with the wisdom and power of His Word. God's Word, the Bible, is our arsenal, containing all the weapons we need to win the crucial battle for our minds.

One of the great things about being alive in these times is the number of sources for acquiring the truth of God's Word. We have Web sites, Christian music, youth groups, youth conferences, guest speakers, radio and TV stations, instructional CDs and DVDs, and books. These resources make it possible to "abide" in God's Word—that means keep absorbing it and applying it in your life.

Need a couple more weapons? Try praise and prayer. Praise kicks the devil's tail every time. He can't stand to hear it. It's like Freddy Krueger's metal talons scraping down the blackboard of his mind. It makes him cringe, cover his ears, and curl into a fetal position, hoping it will go away. But this praise must be real, from the heart. You can't go through the motions—raise your hands just to mimic someone else—or mindlessly mouth the words to a praise chorus.

The same thing goes with prayer. It's gotta be real. Some people breeze through the Lord's Prayer the same way they recite the Big Mac jingle. God doesn't want you to sing Him a jingle. He wants words to spring from the depths of your heart. He wants you to keep it real. And He wants prayers inspired by your close relationship with Him.

You should approach God in prayer as your loving Father. He adores you. He is full of mercy, and He wants to help you. Think about that: Some people help you out of duty or guilt—or so that you will help them someday. Not God. He really wants to help you. He would absolutely love the opportunity to help you.

Next, get to know Jesus. If you have one of those "red-letter" Bibles, go through it and read every single word Jesus said. You'll learn that Jesus is your wise and true Friend. He loves you so much that He died for you.

Finally, get to know God's Holy Spirit living inside you. (And if you're not sure God's Spirit is part of the fabric of your inner being, all you have to do is ask. Right now would be fine.)

God's Spirit can help you pray even when you can't find the

right words, or any words at all. The Spirit can translate the deep-
est feelings in your soul—feelings you can't put into words or
even describe—and convey them to God the Father. Having the
Holy Spirit in you is like having your own personal prayer inter-
preter.

If you would like some inspiration and instruction on prayer,
the Bible is full of them. Check out Psalms, for example. This
book of the Bible provides dozens of prayers—from heartfelt
praises, to anguished cries for help, to dead-honest confessions of
sin.

Mary needs to use these weapons. As she approaches God in
prayer, she will be able to take a wrecking ball to all those strongholds in her mind. The truth of God's Word and the reality of His
power will set her free.

She will see the truth: That her stepdad is doing the best he
can to be a good father to her and a good husband to her mom.
That living as a blended family isn't easy, and that everyone needs
to show mercy and understanding and compassion to everyone
else. That tantrums and disobedience aren't the way to bring
about positive change.

John's Got a Problem: "My stepdaughter won't give me a chance!"

Now, let's take a look at another key player in this family drama.
Just because John is an adult doesn't mean that he isn't part of
the problem.

John knows that he needs to take the leadership position in his
family, but Mary is wearing him down. He's tired of the screaming fights, the slamming doors, and the icy stares. He's grown
weary of setting up boundaries that Mary is going to leap over

anyway. Lately, he just comes home from work, turns on ESPN, and lapses into a sports coma.

John is hiding from his responsibility, because, at heart, he hates confrontation—especially when nothing good seems to come from it. He has begun telling himself, *Well, if I just stay off of Mary's case for a while, our problems will work themselves out. In time, she'll come to accept me. Of course, I'll keep praying about it, but beyond that, what can I do?*

Did you catch that last part? John is excusing himself from taking real action, and he's using prayer as an *excuse*. Now, you've already read that prayer is a great weapon for battling Satan—but *not* if it's used as an excuse for shrugging off responsibility. If you misuse prayer like this, it's allowing Satan to turn one of your own weapons against you!

At this point in the John/Mary saga, I should clarify what I mean when I say that John should assume his God-given position in the home. I don't mean that he should try to be Mr. Macho, ranting and raving like a TV drill sergeant. The Bible teaches that a man should love his family in the same way that Christ loves His people, the Church. And Christ was an effective leader, but He was also a humble servant. He put others' needs ahead of His own comfort.

So, like Christ, John needs to take firm, loving responsibility for his family, including Mary. He should reassure her that even though the divorce has been painful to her, she can throw herself into God's loving arms and trust that her stepdad is doing his best to be a loving, responsible parent to her. John also needs to assure her that he had nothing to do with the divorce—that he came along after the fact and is just trying to be the best husband and parent he can.

John's task isn't easy. Like Mary, he also has territory in his mind that has become occupied by the enemy. John was verbally abused as a child. His domineering mother had a sharp tongue and frequently said things like, "John, you are such an incompetent mess! How do you expect to ever get a good job and be a good husband and father, huh? You're a slacker, and you're never going to get anywhere in life!"

John tried hard to please his mom, because he craved her approval. But the harder he tried, the more mistakes he made. He had a habit of being clumsy, so his mother told him all the time that he was a klutz. And, as you might guess, he dropped *more* things and ran into more things because he was so nervous, especially around her.

His clumsiness and poor self-esteem made it hard for him to make friends. Then, in high school, there was a girl he really liked. They had a few dates, but she ended up dumping him for another guy, one who practically glowed with confidence and competence.

Every rejection, harsh word, and disappointment became another brick in a satanic stronghold in John's mind. Soon, he had no courage or optimism for life. He became shy, quiet, and withdrawn. He tried to adapt to life by being as low-key as possible. He told himself, *There's no point in telling people what you're thinking or what you want, because they won't listen anyway. If you want people to accept you, you better go along with whatever they want.*

Sure, when he first became a parent, John tried to stand his ground and fulfill his responsibilities, but Mary only hated him for it. She attacked him verbally, just as his mother used to do. He became afraid that he would "lose" Mary, just like his friends and high-school sweetheart, so he eventually gave up. *At least if I give Mary what she wants,* he reasoned, *she'll quit screaming at me. Besides, I'm not going to win in this situation anyway, so why make things miserable in the process?*

Can you imagine what John and Mary's home life is like? Can you picture the strife? True, at the moment, the verbal sparring has stopped, but strife doesn't always equal open warfare. Many times, strife is an angry undercurrent in a home. Everyone knows it's there, but nobody wants to deal with it—or even acknowledge its existence.

This home's atmosphere is bleak, and the devil loves it.

What do you think will happen to Mary, and her mom and stepdad—three well-meaning Christian people trapped in a battle zone? Will they make it? It would be a shame to see another marriage fail and another family fall to ruin.

They can make it, but it won't be up to a family counselor or their pastor. It's up to the family. They will need to take John 8:31 and 32 to heart. ("If you hold to my teaching, you are really my disciples. Then you will know the truth, and the truth will set you free.") They will need to continue to study God's Word to discern His truth. Then they will need to act on that truth to set them free from their destructive patterns. They will all have to confront their pasts and realize why they feel and act the way they do.

It's painful to face our pasts, our faults, then deal with them. As a rule, people prefer to justify their misbehavior and negative attitudes. They allow their pasts—how they were raised, etc.—to pollute the rest of their lives. This doesn't work, and it's not fair to the people in our lives. Like some of you, I was abused when I was young. I was abused emotionally, verbally, and sexually. So I understand that the past might explain *why* we suffer. But we can't use the past as an *excuse* to stay in bondage to a negative, defeatist approach to life.

Jesus stands ready to fulfill the biblical promise to set you free. He will lead you to freedom in any area of your life, if only you're willing to follow Him. I am living proof of that truth.

A Winnable War

No temptation has seized you except what is common to man. And God is
faithful; he will not let you be tempted beyond what you can bear. But when
you are tempted, he will also provide a way out.
—1 Corinthians 10:13

I hope that the story of John and Mary shows you how Satan can use our life circumstances to build strongholds in our minds, to invade our minds one sector, one level, at a time.

Thank God that we have weapons to lay waste to every single one of these strongholds. God won't abandon us in the heat of battle. Remember always the truth of 1 Corinthians 10:13: God won't ever let you be overmatched in battle. You will be able to bear any temptation Satan tosses your way. God will always provide a way out of trouble—an escape route for you.

No matter what battle you're facing now—or what might come your way in the future—God is on your side. And that means you can't lose.

CHAPTER 3

Just Who Do You Think You Are?

For as he thinks in his heart, so is he . . .
—Proverbs 23:7 NKJV

Think about the words in that verse; it's one of the most important verses in the entire Bible! That's why you'll see it sprinkled throughout this book. Your thoughts are powerful. They aren't just images and attitudes that lurk in your head; they determine who you are, and who you are going to become. Given this reality, shouldn't you make thinking the right kind of thoughts a top priority in your life?

In this chapter, I want to impress on you the absolute necessity of getting your thought life in synch with God's Word. Because here is an unshakable truth about life: You can't live a positive life if you have a negative mind.

Romans 8:5 warns us, "Those who live according to the sinful nature have their minds set on what that nature desires; but those who live in accordance with the Spirit have their minds set on what the Spirit desires."

Let me put this truth another way: If your mental road map is filled with negativity, greed, lust, and pride, you will not be able to follow the path that God has laid out for your life's journey. You are going to stumble down ravines, charge into dead ends, and take detours that will lead you to disaster.

Do you see people around you whose lives seem to be a perpetual mess? Do a few of your friends fit into this category? Maybe it's a brother or sister. People try to help them; maybe they try to help themselves, but they just can't make any consistent progress. If so, it is probably because their efforts are well-meant but ultimately ineffective. For example, if someone is addicted to methamphetamine, those around him might think that if they can control his access to the drug, things will be okay. This approach might help for a while, but addicts are crafty and resourceful. If they really want to find drugs, they probably will.

The only way to truly help someone like this is to get his mind straightened out—then his life will follow. You have to get to the root of the problem, not just deal with the visible results.

I'll give you a sneak preview of an interview you'll read later in this chapter. The interview features Terrence, a young man who was once addicted to drugs. As he tells of how he destroyed this particular stronghold in his life, he explains that he didn't merely quit using drugs. He says, "I became a new person. I became the kind of person who wouldn't use drugs."

He changed his whole way of thinking, his entire attitude toward life and drugs. That's why he is drug-free today, while so many others are trapped in a heartbreaking cycle of rebound/relapse/repeat.

The Lord impressed this truth on me years ago, as I struggled to have personal fellowship with Him, through prayer and reading and studying the Bible. I was having a terrible time disciplining myself to do these things—until God showed me how important they are to life. He showed me that just as my physical life depends on nourishment, exercise, and proper medical care, my spiritual life thrives on spending regular, high-quality time with my loving Creator.

By helping me understand this parallel between physical and spiritual well-being, God helped me give fellowship with Him priority status in my life. Now I have a whole different attitude toward maintaining and growing my spiritual life. I wouldn't ignore the pangs of physical hunger, because I understand that eating isn't just a "routine" that I feel like I should go through; it's something I *need*. Feeding myself spiritually is vital, too. In fact, it's *more* important than the physical. After all, as it's been said, "We are not human beings having a spiritual experience; we are spiritual beings having a human experience."

The War on Drugs, a Front-Line Interview

Check out this interview with Terrence, a young man who was once addicted to drugs. Note the mind-set that got him into drugs—and the one that helped him find a way out.

How did you get addicted to drugs in the first place?

It was like falling down a hole. It happened so fast that I didn't even realize I was falling. One minute, I was at a party, listening to some music with a few new friends; the next minute I was desperate—doing things I never thought I'd do in a million years—all for the next high. There was no hideous thing I wouldn't do. Within weeks, I hated drugs. I hated getting high, but I had to.

What was drug addiction like?

It was like a trap, and I felt so stupid because I walked into it willingly. I was a smart kid. I knew the dangers. But I chose them anyway. I thought, *Other guys can't handle it, but I'm smart. I'm strong. I can stop. I'll be careful. I'll be able to control it.* And then, as soon as I started using, I knew I'd been taken.

So, you lost control?

I never really had control from the moment I chose to step over the line and get messed up for the first time. You don't want to panic, so you tell yourself, *It's cool. This isn't so bad. I'm just like all these other people.* But the truth is that you're dying and you know it, like, ten seconds after you start. And that's about nine seconds too late.

How did you stop doing drugs?

I didn't just stop using drugs. I became a new person. I'm still becoming that person every day, actually. I can't stop running in the opposite direction from [drugs] or it just might catch me. God has helped me a lot to change my identity. I said I was a Christian before I got into drugs, but I wasn't living it. I wasn't a new creation. I'd say to anyone out there, if you have an addiction or a bad habit, don't just stop the behavior; change your whole identity. Become somebody else—someone who would never do the destructive things you are doing. Change your friends if they're into drugs. I did. I changed jobs, locations, habits, my thinking, the way I talked and dressed. Anything that fed my old ways.

What would you say to readers who are thinking of experimenting—or trying drugs "just once."

I thought just one little time wouldn't hurt. That one time led to thousands of wasted dollars, one hospitalization, almost dying, and years of regret. One little time won't hurt? I have just one word for that: OUCH!

Is Your Fruit Ripe?

In the gospel of Matthew, Jesus explained that a tree is known by its fruit. A diseased tree is going to bear bad fruit. An immature or malnourished tree won't bear any fruit at all.

The same principle rings true in our lives. Thoughts bear fruit. Think good thoughts, and the fruit of your life will be good. Think bad thoughts, and the fruit in your life will be bad.

You can take note of someone's attitude and demeanor toward life and know what kind of thinking is behind it. A sweet, kind person is not filled with mean, vindictive thoughts. By the same token, a truly evil person doesn't spend every waking hour dwelling on pure, loving thoughts.

Memorize Proverbs 23:7, perhaps in one or more Bible translations. One of my favorites is from the *New American Standard Bible*, which says, "For as he thinks within himself, so he is." But whichever version you prefer, hold on to the core message of this verse and let it be a guiding force in your life. As you think you are in your heart, so you will be. In other words, see it, then be it.

CHAPTER 4

Perseverance = Payoff

Let us not become weary in doing good, for at the proper
time we will reap a harvest if we do not give up.

—Galatians 6:9

Right now, you might think your life stinks. You might be lonely, struggling in school, feeling rejected by your parents and friends. Maybe, like me, you've been a victim of abuse by someone (like my father) whom you thought you could trust and you don't know how to deal with your feelings of guilt, betrayal, and worthlessness. I'm here to tell you one thing: Don't give up!

No matter how bad your life is messed up and out of control, you can regain the turf the devil has stolen from you. You might have to do it an inch at a time, but, by leaning on God's grace and power every step of the way, you can have a life beyond your best dreams.

That's what the apostle Paul is saying in that verse at the beginning of the chapter—keep on keeping on! Don't quit! And Paul earned the right to say those words. Many times he was chained up in a jail cell. He survived brutal beatings. He also survived a shipwreck and a bite from a poisonous snake. Beyond all that, he had some type of physical condition that tormented him so much that he begged God three times to take it away. So, this isn't some overprivileged wimp urging you to persevere. This is a true survivor.

What got Paul through his challenges—and what'll get you through, too—is relying on God's strength. In the book of Isaiah, God promises, "When you pass through the waters, I will be with you; and through the rivers, they shall not overflow you" (Isaiah 43:2 NKJV). Whatever you go through, God will be with you, loving you, listening to you, encouraging you, and giving you the spiritual strength to endure.

The Choice Is Yours

Have you ever heard the expression "A penny for your thoughts"? Well, if someone actually makes you that offer, you should take him or her up on it. You could get rich pretty quick. Over the next 24 hours, your mind could generate as many as 50,000 thoughts—often several at a time. So, one day's worth of thoughts could bring you $500!

The problem is that many of those thoughts aren't worth even a penny. Today, if we aren't careful, our thoughts can be sparked by unwholesome images on the Internet or TV, bad advice, and careless talk from celebrities. So much bad information is bombarding you 24/7 that it takes little or no effort to think the wrong kind of thoughts. It's like the default mode on a computer. No one says, "Hmmm, I'm bored, so I think that I will create some bad thoughts in my mind and amuse myself with them for a while." With the many tools Satan has at his disposal, all you have to do is sit there passively, and, in no time, something bad will visit your mind. You don't have to go hunting for stuff that's bad for your mind; it will come to you.

Good and right thoughts, on the other hand, take effort. You have to *choose* to think God's way, then continue to choose right thoughts every day and every night. Remember that interview with Terrence, the former drug addict? He said that the process of "becoming a new person" was something he worked on every day.

Think of it this way: If you want to get out of shape physically, you really don't have to *do* anything. Just sitting around and eating whatever junk food happens to be handy will soon turn you into a weak doughboy (or dough-girl).

But to be healthy and strong takes vigilant effort. You must think about what you're going to eat—and what to avoid. You have to make smart food choices at every meal, at every snack time. You can't allow yourself to fall into careless eating habits. And you have to discipline yourself to exercise—make it a priority in your life. You're going to have to do things when you don't feel like it.

Your mind deserves the same kind of attention—in fact, it deserves even more attention. You will face many choices in life. God wants you to make the right choices, and that starts in your mind. Your thoughts become your words; your thoughts become your actions. Your thoughts become your life. So, choose life-affirming, life-generating thoughts. When you do, positive words and positive actions will follow. Live your life expecting the best, not fearing the worst. And remember that you are not alone. Keep telling yourself, "I won't give up, because God is on my side. He loves me, and He will always help me." Remember forever this promise from the Bible: "The Lord is watching his children, listening to their prayers" (1 Peter 3:12 TLB).

Don't Give Up—A Mind Isn't Built in a Day

As you strive to persevere and think and act the right way, you will get discouraged sometimes. That shouldn't be a surprise. Remember, you're trying to reprogram a mind that's been corrupted by all kinds of worldly "viruses" and "worms."

You're going to have to let go of some stuff. You're going to have to be patient. And once things are fixed, you are going to have to learn a few new commands, take a few extra precautions.

But take heart; you have God, the ultimate IT guy, on your side. He can reprogram your mental hard drive, clean up the viruses, and install firewalls to protect you in the future. Sometimes this process takes time, but I promise you this: It's worth it.

CHAPTER

5

The Power of the Positive

L ife isn't easy, but it is simple. Positive minds produce positive lives. Negative minds produce negative lives. And positive minds are always filled with faith and hope, while negative minds are full of fear and doubt.

Are you afraid to hope? Are you afraid to imagine what cool things might happen in your life—because you can't face the disappointment of seeing those hopes crumble? A lot of people feel that way. They have been disappointed so many times that they don't want to open themselves up to another hurt. They are living life by playing defense all of the time. Their focus is protect, protect, protect.

It's understandable that people want to avoid the pain of disappointment, but let's go back to that key verse, Proverbs 23:7: "For as [a person] thinks in his heart, so is he" (NKJV).

I want to confess something to you: Years ago, I was an extremely negative person. If you've seen me on TV or heard me speak, you might find this hard to believe, but it's true. I used to say, "If I thought two positive thoughts in a row, my brain would cramp up!" Here was my life philosophy: "If you don't expect anything good to happen, then you won't be disappointed when it doesn't."

As you might imagine, I was a *real* party to be around.

I thought the way I did because I had endured so many disappointments in life—including being abused and not being able to go to college. These disappointments colored my whole outlook on life. My thoughts were negative; my words were negative. My whole life was negative.

To try and pull myself out of the quicksand of negativity, I began to seriously study God's Word. I prayed that God would restore me, restore my soul. As I made these efforts, I realized that my negative attitude toward life had to go.

I focused on verses like Matthew 8:13, in which Jesus tells us that as we think and believe, "it will be done for us . . ." This made perfect sense. Every belief I had was negative, so it was no wonder that negative things happened to me all the time.

Now, it's important to point out that Jesus isn't saying that you can get anything you want just by thinking about it. God is your Lord, not your personal genie in a bottle. But, He does have a perfect plan for you. And that plan isn't for you to go through your life depressed and discouraged. Jesus proclaimed, "I have come that they may have life, and that they may have it more abundantly" (John 10:10 NKJV).

If you don't have a clue what God wants you to do with your life at this point, that's okay. Pray to Him about it. Say, "God I don't know what Your plan is for me, but I know that You love me and that whatever You do with my life, it'll be good. Please guide me in the abundant life I know You want me to live."

Then practice being positive in each situation that arises in your life. That won't be easy, because not everything that happens to you will be positive; not everything will be good. But you can expect God to bring good out of even bad circumstances. He can even bring joy out of sad circumstances.

Now, I know that the whole "when life gives you lemons, make lemonade" thing looks good on paper. But does it work in real life? Can God really work all things for good, as He promises in Romans 8:28?

The answer is yes. And here's just one example, from the brutal world of boxing. Gene Tunney was a great heavyweight boxer, with knockout power in both hands. Unfortunately, the many rounds of pummeling hardheaded opponents eventually turned Tunney's fists to kindling. He broke so many bones in his hands that it looked like his career was over. Many fighters would have given up, if they were in Tunney's shoes—or boxing boots, in this case.

But Tunney didn't quit. He stayed positive. He reprogrammed his entire approach to his sport. He changed his style, from that of a hard-swinging brawler to a technically precise tactician who specialized in strategy. He focused on well-placed jabs rather than wild haymakers. Tunney's new scientific style served him well. He eventually earned a world championship bout with Jack "The Manassa Mauler" Dempsey, the most feared heavyweight of his day.

Tunney took Dempsey apart. Twice. A brawler, Dempsey was frustrated by Tunney's careful, deliberate style. If Tunney had tried to fight Dempsey using his old style, he would have gotten rocked. He couldn't have stood toe-to-toe and traded knockout punches with Dempsey. So, a seeming tragedy in Tunney's life became the very thing that helped him realize his dream.

You might be more familiar with the saga of Lance Armstrong, who overcame life-threatening cancer to become the greatest cyclist of his generation. He is on record as saying, "Cancer is the best thing that ever happened to me." He has said that he would never have become a multiple Tour de France winner without the perspective and perseverance he learned while battling cancer.

Like Tunney and Armstrong, you can adjust to what life hurls at you. You don't have to fall apart when things don't work out the way you hope. Trust God to work good in your circumstances. You just might find that your final results will be even better than what you'd hoped!

A final point on this topic: If you tend to be a negative person, don't feel bad about it. Don't feel condemned. Because condemnation itself is negative. There's nothing worse than feeling negative about your negativism—on top of everything else! Just recognize the problem and begin to trust God to restore you, to show you the way out of your dark tunnel.

A New Day!

Therefore if any person is [ingrafted] in Christ (the Messiah) he is a new creation (a new creature altogether); the old [previous moral and spiritual condition] has passed away. Behold, the fresh and new has come!
—2 Corinthians 5:17 AMP

Even if you have been a negative person in the past, you don't have to remain a negative person. If you believe in Christ, you are a new person, a new creation. You don't have to let the stuff that happened to you in the past keep dragging you down. You can have a whole new kind of life. You can have your mind renewed by the power and wisdom of God's Word. So take heart—good things are going to happen to you.

One of the hardest things about being set free from the prison of negativity is facing the truth: "I've been a negative person, but I want to change. I don't have the power to change myself, but I believe God will change me as I trust Him. This will take time, but I'm not going to get discouraged with myself. God has begun a good work in me, and He is well able to bring it to full completion" (see Philippians 1:6).

God's Holy Spirit, living inside you, is key to bringing things to completion in your life. If you are willing to listen and be spiritually aware, the Holy Spirit will warn you each time you start sinking back into negativity—kind of like that "Empty" light in your car that comes on when your fuel tank is running dry. Heed the warning. Ask God for help. Don't think you can handle this yourself. Let Him fill your tank.

Here's something interesting that will happen to you as you let God transform the negative you into a more positive version: You will notice negativity in other people, and you won't like it. You'll wonder, *Was I really that negative once?* It's like this: I smoked cigarettes for many years before finally quitting. But once I quit, I couldn't even stand the smell of cigarette smoke.

I'm the same way toward negativity. I was a very negative person. I could walk into a beautiful new home that was immaculately decorated—and notice the one corner of wallpaper that was coming loose, or the one tiny smudge on a window. Now I can't stand negativism. It's almost offensive to me.

It's important to note here that being positive doesn't equal being unrealistic, with a big dopey grin on our faces all the time. If you have the flu, don't say, "I'm not sick at all," or "I really like having a burning fever and puking in the toilet all day—it's fun!"

Don't deny the truth, but do stay positive. Say, "I believe God is going to heal me; this bug isn't going to hold me down for long." Isn't that better than, "I'll never feel better. In fact, I'll probably get worse and end up in the hospital."

In other words, strive for balance in life. Have a "ready mind," one that is prepared to keep life in perspective and deal effectively with whatever happens.

Have you heard the phrase "ready mind" before? It comes from the book of Acts, chapter 17, which talks about a group of people who received information with "readiness of mind." This means having our minds open to God's will for us—no matter what that will might be.

Have you ever experienced the pain of a romantic breakup? Recently, a young woman I know faced the sorrow of a broken engagement. After she and her boyfriend called off the engagement, they began praying about whether the Lord wanted them to keep dating, even though marriage was no longer in the immediate future.

The woman wanted the relationship to continue, and she sincerely hoped and believed that her ex-fiancé would feel the same way.

I advised her, "Have a ready mind, in case things don't work out the way you want them to."

She countered, "Well, isn't that being negative?"

No, it wasn't. Negativism would be thinking, *My engagement is broken; my life is over. No one will ever want me again. I'm unlovable, and I've failed at love. I guess now I'll end up being a miserable old lady with about thirty cats!*

Having a positive, ready mind, on the other hand, would produce this attitude: "I'm truly sad about this broken engagement, but I'm going to trust God to help me deal with the aftermath. I hope my boyfriend and I can still date. I'm going to ask for, and believe, that our relationship will be restored. But, more than anything else, I want God's perfect will. If things don't turn out the way I want them to, I'll survive, because Jesus lives in me. Dealing with this situation may be hard for a while, but I trust the Lord. I believe that in the end, everything will work out for the best."

This is how you face facts and remain positive.

This is balance.

The Power of Hope

My husband, Dave, and I believe that Joyce Meyer Ministries and the work we do will grow each year. We always want to help more and more people. But we also realize that if God has a different plan, we cannot let that situation steal our joy.

In other words, we hope for many things, but more important than all the things we hope *for* is the One we hope *in*. We don't know if our ministry will continue to grow or hit a plateau, or even diminish in size or scope. But we do know that, whatever the case, God will always work things out for our good.

Some of you might be saying at this point, "Joyce, if you knew my situation, even you wouldn't expect me to be positive."

If you feel this way, I want to share a story with you. Way back in Old Testament times, God promised a man named Abraham that he would be "the father of many nations." That his descendants would be so many that you couldn't count them all.

There was only one problem: Abraham was about 100 years old at the time, and his wife, Sarah, was ancient, too, way past those prime child-bearing years. The Bible account goes so far as to say her womb was "deadened."

So, Abraham sized up his situation. He was an old guy with an old wife—and Geritol, and all the rest hadn't been invented yet. There were no test-tube babies in Abraham's time. There weren't any test tubes, period. Human reason said the situation was impossible, but the Bible says that old Abe didn't waver or distrust God's promise. He simply hoped in faith. He left the situation in God's hands, realizing that, humanly speaking, he had no reason for optimism. So he put everything in God's miracle-working realm.

The lesson for you? Even when things seem impossible, don't discount that God will sometimes step in and do something amazing. You shouldn't expect miracles all of the time. But it's okay for you to believe God for them when He has told you to do so. Miracles do happen for those who really believe.

Isaiah 30:18 is one of my favorite Scriptures: "Yet the LORD longs to be gracious to you; he rises to show you compassion." Meditate on these words, and they will bring you great hope. God is looking for someone to be gracious to. He wants to show His goodness. But someone with a sour attitude and a dark mind, isn't going to experience this blessing.

Don't Let Satan Put
Your Mind in a Bind

t's confession time for me again: At one point in my Christian
life, I began to struggle to believe certain things. I began to
question whether what I was doing with my life and ministry
was really what God wanted me to do. I sensed that I was losing
sight of the vision God had given me for Joyce Meyer Ministries.
As a result, I grew miserable. Doubt and lack of belief always produce misery.

Then, for two days in a row, a phrase came to me: *mind-binding spirits.* The first time *mind-binding spirits* popped into my head, I didn't give it much thought. But the words kept coming back to me.

I thought about all the tricks and strategies that Satan uses against believers, to confuse and cloud and pollute their minds. So, I began to pray—for the defeat of mind-binding spirits, in my own life and for the whole body of Christ. After only a couple minutes of praying, I felt a tremendous sense of relief, of being rescued from an attack on my mind. It was a dramatic feeling, and I was grateful for the sense of release God gave to me.

Now, you might be asking, "What in the world are 'mind-binding spirits'? Sounds like something from a fantasy novel."

Think of the concept this way: Mind-binding spirits are like tiny seeds that Satan plants in your mind. In time, these seeds sprout into weeds, weeds of doubt, insecurity, unbelief, and cynicism. They pollute and clutter the landscape of your mind. They coil around your mind, squeezing it, irritating it. You begin to feel miserable.

If you feel these kinds of weeds sprouting and growing in your mind, it's time to take out your spiritual weed-whacker—by believing and confessing God's Word. In John 8, Jesus promised, "If you abide (continue) in My word . . . you are truly My disciples. And you will know the Truth, and the Truth will set you free" (verses 31-32 AMP).

In other words, the Word of the Lord can make your mind weed-free. That's what it did for me. Before Satan began to put my mind in a bind, I believed that even though I was a woman from Fenton, Missouri, who didn't come from a high-profile background, God could still use me to bring good to the world. He would open doors for me, and I would preach all over the world, sharing the practical, liberating messages He had given me. I also believed that I would have a radio ministry, that God would use me to heal the sick, and that Dave's and my children would be used in ministry, as well. I believed all of these things—and many other wonderful things God had placed in my heart.

Then the satanic attack came. After a while, I couldn't seem to believe much of anything. I began to tell myself, *I probably just made up those dreams about a ministry. It probably won't ever happen.*

But after I prayed, those spirits, those weeds, vanished. And once they were gone, the ability to believe the best for my life and ministry came rushing back in.

Decide to Believe

When they hear the word *believe*, some people associate it with an emotion. But while belief can carry emotions with it, it's more than a feeling. Belief is a decision, an act of the will. Belief is persevering and following God's plan even when our emotions are ragged, even when our minds lack understanding. Belief goes beyond understanding. It's following the conviction of your heart, even when your mind is lagging behind, or arguing with itself. It's important to understand this true definition of belief, because our minds often refuse to believe what they cannot understand.

Note that because God's ways are higher than our ways, and His understanding is so much greater than ours, it is crucial to believe what His Word says, even if we don't fully understand all of the whys and whens and hows. If you're reading this book at night, look at the lights around you. Do you understand all of the intricacies of electricity and circuitry that create the light around you? Probably not. But you can still enjoy it and benefit from the illumination.

Think back to our Abraham story. If he looked only at the physical realities, the cold, hard medical facts, he would have no reason to believe God's promise to him. But he believed God instead, and his belief was richly rewarded: He is the forefather of the entire Jewish people. Whether in person or via the media, you probably see some of Abraham's descendants every single day.

The devil has plenty of seeds he wants to plant in your mind. But you have the power, through belief in God's Word and His love and power, to chop 'em off, yank 'em out, or keep them from taking root in the first place.

Teen True or False

Put your mind to the test with the following quiz . . .
1. Most teens who drink do so responsibly.
2. Among teens, virgins are still a strong majority.
3. TV and other forms of entertainment have little or no effect on sexual behavior.
4. A significant number of kids are having sex by age 13.
5. It's not uncommon for a U.S. teen to have as many as four credit cards.
6. Condoms are an effective way to prevent pregnancy and STDs.
7. Today's teens and young adults are very concerned about STDs.
8. Most sexually active young people have condoms on hand.
9. The dangers of marijuana are exaggerated. It's really not that harmful.
10. If you're under 16, it's illegal to have sexual intercourse.
11. You can't get an STD unless you have sexual intercourse.
12. Most sexually active women don't get an STD.
13. Parents are a major source from which teens get their alcohol.

[answers to Teen True or False quiz]

1. **False.** Almost 50 percent of people under the age of twenty-one who drink alcohol, binge-drink, meaning they consume five or more drinks in a four-hour period.[1]

2. **False.** Half of all ninth- through twelfth-graders have had sexual intercourse.[2]

3. **False.** Teens who watch a lot of sex on TV are more than twice as likely to have sex as those whose TV-sex viewing is restricted.[3]

4. **True.** According to the U.S. Centers for Disease Control and *Prevention's* latest Youth Risk Behavior study, 7.4 percent of kids have had sexual intercourse by the time they turn 13.[4]

5. **True.** Almost 20 percent of eighteen-year-olds have four or more credit cards—with an average balance of between $3,000 and $7,000.[5]

6. **False.** For example, half of the people visiting a Colorado STD clinic reported condom-use mishaps, such as slippage, breakage, or improper use. Additionally, only 46 percent of sexually active young adults "always," or even "often" use condoms during sexual activity. And only 36 percent say they always refuse sex if their partners refuse to use a condom.[6]

7. **False.** Forty-four percent of sexually active young people are not concerned about contracting an STD—49 percent of men and 39 percent of women.[7]

8. **False.** While 77 percent of sexually active young men and women say it's smart to carry condoms, only 23 percent say they always have one on hand.[8]

9. **False.** Young people who use marijuana weekly have double the risk of depression later in life—and are three times more likely than non-users to have suicidal thoughts. One factor in these dangers is that today's marijuana is twice as potent as that of previous generations, and today's teens are starting with the drug at younger and younger ages—during crucial brain-development years.[9]

10. **True.** It's illegal to have sex if you're under sixteen—even if your partner is underage, too.[10]

11. **False.** You can get an STD from oral sex, or even hand-to-genital contact.[11]

12. **False.** Eighty percent of sexually active women contract HPV, a sexually transmitted virus that lives on the skin around the vagina, anus, or penis. The approximately thirty strains of HPV are spread by skin-to-skin contact and can cause genital warts and cervical cancer.[12]

13. **True.** In a national survey of more than 700 thirteen- to eighteen-year-olds, "one's own parents"—with their knowledge and consent—was named the number one source for getting alcoholic beverages. "Someone else's parents" (also with knowledge and consent) represented the number four source.[13]

Think About What
You're Thinking About

I will meditate on Your precepts and have respect to
Your ways [the paths of life marked out by Your law].
—Psalm 119:15 AMP

What are the Internet, TV, and music rules in your house? Are there parental controls on your computer? Are there certain TV programs—or entire channels—you're not allowed to watch?

Do you hear "What's it rated?" every time you ask a parent to go see a movie?

Or maybe you have adopted some rules of your own. Maybe

you won't buy a CD with a "Parental Advisory" sticker on it or visit certain Web sites or chat rooms.

If any of this sounds familiar, good for you (and your parent or parents, too)! As media content has become increasingly questionable, more and more people are being careful about what they watch, read, and hear.

Unfortunately, very few people apply the same kind of discipline to their thought lives.

Most people let random thoughts drift into their minds and spend valuable time considering them. Some thoughts are rather innocuous, such as, *I wonder what the world record is for eating hot dogs.* Others can be impure or devious. In any case, careless thoughts distract us from pure thoughts, positive thoughts—thoughts that lead to a rewarding life, rather than a wasted life.

The psalmist, quoted at the beginning of this chapter, understood the concept of "thinking about what you're thinking about." He said he thought about, meditated on, God's guidance. That means he spent loads of time pondering and considering God's character, God's rules for living.

Meditating on God's Word has its rewards. The Bible promises that the person who follows this practice is like a tree firmly planted near streams of water. A tree that produces good fruit and prospers. This kind of person, the Bible promises, will be blessed.

Mark's Gospel puts it another way: "Be careful what you are hearing. The measure [of thought and study] you give [to the truth you hear] will be the measure [of virtue and knowledge] that comes back to you—and more [besides] will be given to you who hear" (Mark 4:24 AMP). In other words, the more time we spend thinking about the Word as we read and hear it, the more power we will have to live out our faith. You get out of God's Word what you put into it.

For example, you've probably heard sermons and songs about caring for "the least of these." You might have thought, *That's a nice sentiment, a good idea. We really should care for people less fortunate than ourselves. Hmm, I wonder what's on TV right now?*

When this kind of thing happens, you have to discipline your mind. You have to meditate on God's Word, not just let it drift through your mind, like smoke.

According to the trusty old Webster's dictionary, the word *meditate* means to reflect on something, to ponder it, to contemplate it—or to intend in your mind to do something. In short, if you want to follow God's Word in your life, you must spend dedicated time thinking about God's message to His people. You have to practice thinking about God's Word, just as you would practice for a sport, musical performance, or a speech.

The book of Joshua urges people to meditate on God's law day and night (see 1:8). That's because this discipline is so important that it shouldn't be crammed into a tiny corner of your busy day.

Take a few moments right now to estimate how much time of your life is spent on contemplating God's Word and thinking about how to apply it to your everyday life. If you're like most people, your meditation time is tiny compared to your TV-watching time, your cell-phone time, and your Web-surfing time.

Here's another question for you: Are you having problems in any areas of your life? If you are, an honest answer to the "how-much-meditation-time" question might disclose the reason why. I know this from personal experience. For most of my life, I didn't think about what I was thinking about. I went to church for years, but never actually thought about what I heard. All the sermons, the songs, and the personal testimonies flew through my head without ever landing and making an impression.

I read the Bible, too—every day. But I never thought about what I was reading. It was just a mindless routine; I wasn't *attending to* the Word. I wasn't devoting thought and study to what I was hearing, and I wasn't putting it into practice.

Instead, I simply thought about whatever happened to pop into my head at any given time. Here's the scary thing: At the time, I didn't know that Satan could inject thoughts into my mind, like a drug. As a result, my mind was filled with satanic lies, as well as just a bunch of nonsense—stuff that wasn't necessarily evil, but just not worth spending any time thinking about. These things kept my mind busy, but not in a productive way. So, even though I was a Christian, the devil was controlling my life—because he was controlling my thoughts.

I needed to change my way of thinking. Maybe you do, too.

A turning point for me came when God gave me the message that is the title of this chapter: Think about what you're thinking about.

A Brand-New Mind

Do not conform any longer to the pattern of this world, but be transformed by the renewing of your mind. Then you will be able to test and approve what God's will is—his good, pleasing and perfect will.
—Romans 12:2

In this passage, Paul assures us that we can follow God's good and perfect will for our lives—if we have renewed our minds. How do we do this? We pray that God will help us follow His way of thinking. We meditate and concentrate on God's life-transforming Word all the time. Meditating on God's Word must become as indispensable to our minds as eating is to our bodies and as breathing is to our lungs.

As we are renewed to God's way of thinking, we will be transformed into who God intends.

Let me note right now, however, that right thinking has nothing to do with salvation. That's right. Salvation is based solely on Jesus' death for you on the cross, and His triumphant resurrection from the grave. You trust Jesus; He saves your soul. You go to heaven because you accept Him in faith.

Oddly enough, heaven will have people who didn't live winning, effective lives on earth, people who strayed from God's plan for them. Why? Because they never renewed their minds according to God's Word. Their hearts belonged to Jesus; someone else, though, imprisoned their minds.

For years, I was one of those people. I was truly born again, and there was no doubt I was going to heaven. But I really had no sense of victory in my life, because my mind was continually occupied by the wrong kind of thoughts.

What, then, are the *right* kinds of thoughts?

Something to Think About . . .

Finally, brothers, whatever is true, whatever is noble, whatever is right, whatever is pure, whatever is lovely, whatever is admirable—if anything is excellent or praiseworthy—think about such things.
—Philippians 4:8

Did you know that the Bible provided such detailed instruction on how to direct our thinking? As you strive to think about what you're thinking about, use Philippians 4:8 as a checklist. If you're like me, as you consider a thought that floats into your mind, you might not even get past the first two qualities.

For example, suppose that you find yourself considering trying pot for the first time, or taking your first drink of hard liquor. So, you ask yourself, *If I do this, am I being true to myself—true to who I should be?* And right there, you have your answer.

But suppose you interpret the "true" criteria another way. You might reason that it's *true* that a lot of your friends and/or classmates are ingesting these substances. Okay, even if you give yourself that one, move on to the next step. Is doing a shot of Jack Daniel's *noble?* (One version of the Bible translates this word as "worthy of reverence.") Do you see how efficiently Philippians 4:8 can guide your thought life and your behavior?

Please use this method as you take a mental inventory of your life. Ask yourself, *What have I been thinking about this past week— and how much of my thought life would stand up to the Philippians 4:8 test?*

If you test your thoughts like this, you will find yourself spending more time thinking about stuff that will build you up, not tear you down. If you're full of wrong thoughts, you will be miserable, just as I was. And here's something else I learned from personal experience: When a person is miserable, he or she usually ends up making lots of others miserable, too. And the people you make most miserable are your family and friends—including your girlfriend or boyfriend—the last people in the world you want to bring down.

I'll close this chapter by revealing one of Satan's favorite deceptive tactics. He wants to trick you into thinking that the source of your misery is what's going on *around* you, outside you—in other words, your circumstances and the people in your life.

The Philippians 4:8 Check-Your-Thinking Checklist

Confused about what to think about? Put your thoughts to the following test:
Are they . . .
1. True
2. Noble
3. Right
4. Pure
5. Lovely
6. Admirable
7. Excellent
8. Praiseworthy

Here's the real deal: No thing and no person can make you miserable without your permission. Some of the happiest people I know struggle financially, face a challenging home life, or battle some type of physical affliction.

For many years, I blamed my unhappiness on things other people were doing—or not doing. I blamed my misery on my husband and my kids. *If only they were different*, I thought, *if only they would be more attentive to my needs and help around the house more often, I would be happy.*

Finally, thankfully, I faced the truth: Nothing my family did or didn't do could bring me down if I chose to have the right attitude. My thoughts, not my husband and kids, were making me miserable.

Let me say it one more time: Think about what you're thinking about. If you do this, it's highly likely that you'll uncover the sources of many of your problems. And once you do that, you'll very quickly be on your way to freedom and peace of mind.

PART TWO

How's Your Head?

INTRODUCTION

But we have the mind of Christ (the Messiah) and do hold
the thoughts (feelings and purposes) of His heart.
—1 Corinthians 2:16 AMP

I have a question for you: Where's your head at right now? Were you in a different head-space last week? Last year?

If you're like most people, your mental condition changes drastically. It can be as unpredictable as the weather. One day you might be calm and peaceful. A week later, you're uptight, anxious, and worried about almost everything.

Or, have you ever made a decision—such as signing up for a certain class in school or breaking up with a love interest—then second-guessed yourself right into a panic attack?

More important, have you felt great about your spiritual life for a while, then found yourself slipping? Unable to find the motivation to crack open your Bible? Making excuses for not attending church or youth group? Not praying unless you had some kind of emergency you wanted God to bail you out of?

I've been there, too. At some points in my life I seemed to be able to believe in God and trust His Word almost like it was second nature to me. But at other times, doubt and unbelief haunted me mercilessly. So, I began to ask myself, *What's wrong with me? Is my mind normal? And what, exactly, is normal, anyway?*

I had a judgmental, critical mind, something that should be considered abnormal for a believer. But since my mind had been this way for a major portion of my life, I figured it had to be normal, even though I questioned it at times. After all, it was what I was used to. Besides, as far as I knew then, there was nothing I could do to change my thought life.

I want to point out that I had been a believer for years at this point in my life, but no one had ever taught me about my thought life or given me standards for how my mind should function as a child of God.

Remember, our minds are not born again when we become Christians. Our minds have to be renewed, and this renewal is a process that requires time. So, don't be discouraged—or devastated—when you read the next part of this book. You might discover that your mind isn't in the right condition. That's okay. Recognizing the problem is the first step to getting where you need to be.

Imagine an athlete who thinks he's in pretty good shape. He's worked out a bit during the summer and seems fit compared to most of his buddies. But he shows up for the first day of football practice and finds out that his forty-yard-dash times are way slow. At first, he can't even believe the stopwatch.

Then it's on to the weight room, where he discovers he can't bench-press his body weight even once. The news is sobering, but if this guy wants to make himself into a football player, he now has some information on where he is physically, versus where he needs to be. His world has been rocked some, but the good news is that he knows something he didn't know before. Now he can deal with reality, not some fantasy notions about himself.

In my case, my world got rocked several years ago when I began to get serious about my relationship with the Lord. As I drew closer to Him, He began to reveal to me how so many of my problems were rooted in wrong thinking. In short, my mind was a mess! It's possible that it had never been in the condition it should have been.

This realization overwhelmed me. I began to see that I was addicted to wrong thinking. I would try to fling out the bad thoughts when they came into my mind, but like boomerangs, they flew right back. If you've ever had a friend who tried to kick cigarettes but then kept relapsing and giving in to temptation and the old routine, you get the picture.

It's just plain hard to overcome wrong thinking, because Satan will fight you *aggressively* during the process of renewing your mind. So, you have to pray and study the Bible. You have to grab God's promises and hold on for dear life. You have to press on. If you do this, little by little, you'll reclaim your mind. You'll be mentally wandering less and focusing more. You'll be less upset and confused and more sure of the direction your life is going. You'll be less afraid, because you'll realize that, as a child of God, you have the privilege of casting *all* your cares on Him.

So, prayerfully proceed to the next part of *The Battlefield of the Mind*. I believe it will open your eyes to abnormal mind-sets— and paint a picture of the right-minded follower of Jesus, determined to walk in victory.

Is My Mind
Normal, or What?

The Center for Disease Control estimates that almost two-thirds of American adults are overweight—with 31 percent being so overweight as to be obese. So, if you walk around the mall in your hometown, you might assume that being overweight is normal. It's not. Sure, the average person might be overweight these days, but that is not *normal*.

This distinction between average and normal becomes even more important when we talk about the mind. When you ask yourself, *What condition should my mind be in?* you can't just look at the people around you and compare yourself to them. You have to go deeper.

When we become Christians, God's Holy Spirit takes up residence inside us. Now, the Spirit knows God's mind, and one of His purposes is to reveal to us God's wisdom and guidance.

But we have a challenge as we process the Holy Spirit's direction and His revelations to us. As humans, we are a combo of the natural and the spiritual. The natural brain operates by natural laws—neurons firing, serotonin being released, and so on. The brain's natural functions help us process information, solve problems, and lots, lots more. But for all its wonders, our amazing natural brains don't understand spiritual stuff (see 1 Cor. 2:14).

To grasp the spiritual, the mind needs to be enlightened by the Holy Spirit. The problem is that our minds often give the Spirit a "busy" signal when He is trying to enlighten us. Worry, anxiety, fear, and the like cause that busy signal. When our minds are occupied with stuff like this, they can't be attentive to God's Spirit.

In short, your mind is normal when it's at rest. Not blank, like a computer screen when it's first powered up, but at rest, serene, attentive to God's leading and inspiration.

Think about it for a minute: Is your mind usually, *normally*, serene? Or is its bandwidth overloaded, bombarded with information, stress, demands, deadlines, and schedules? As you'll read elsewhere in this book, 99 percent of teens like you feel stressed at least some of the time, so if you're feeling overwhelmed, you are not alone.

When was the last time you allowed your mind to just chill? To attend to the spiritual side of you, rather than the ever-imposing natural side?

The Holy Spirit stands ready to enrich you with divine wis-

Are You Too Stressed for Success?

Ninety-nine percent of teens feel stressed at least some of the time, and 67 percent feel stress without knowing why.

From a national survey, here are teens' top five stress-inducers. How many of them do you share?

1. Feeling overwhelmed by homework
2. Not having enough money
3. Wanting to do well on college-placement tests
4. Juggling multiple priorities
5. Feeling fat/physically unattractive[1]

---

dom and inspiration, but if your mind is too busy with other things, you will miss out.

Big God, Small Voice

The LORD said [to Elijah], "Go out and stand on the mountain in the presence of the LORD, for the LORD is about to pass by." Then a great and powerful wind tore the mountains apart and shattered the rocks before the LORD, but the LORD was not in the wind. After the wind there was an earthquake, but the LORD was not in the earthquake. After the earthquake came a fire, but the LORD was not in the fire. And after the fire came a gentle whisper.
—1 Kings 19:11-12

Have you experienced anything like Elijah did in this passage? Have you ever prayed for wisdom from God, but He answered in a way you didn't expect?

For years, I prayed for divine revelation from God, through His Spirit living in me. I knew that my requests were in line with the Bible. I felt sure I should be asking God to reveal things to me, and I felt sure I would receive an answer.

But instead, a lot of the time I felt like a spiritual dunce. Then, finally, I learned that I wasn't catching much of what the Holy Spirit was throwing my way because my mind was so frantic and busy that I was missing the insight being offered to me.

Imagine you're at a loud concert with your best friend. Right in the middle of a drum solo, you whisper something. Not only are you going to go unheard, but, unless your friend happens to look at you, she might not even know you're saying anything at all.

That's the way it is with the communication from God's Spirit to our hearts and minds. The ways of the Spirit are gentle. Most of the time, He speaks to us just as in Elijah's case, in a still, small voice. That's why it's vital to keep our minds tuned in to God's frequency.

There's a great gospel spiritual that begins, "I woke up this morning with my mind stayed on Jesus." That's good advice.

Isaiah 26:3 promises, "You will guard him and keep him in perfect and constant peace whose mind [both its inclination and its character] is stayed on You, because he commits himself to You, leans on You, and hopes confidently in You" (AMP).

Commit to keeping your mind at peace. Satan is going to try to overload your circuits and overwork your mind by filling it with evil thoughts, destructive thoughts, and just plain meaningless thoughts. You must keep those circuits open and available to God's Spirit. Keep your mind "stayed on Jesus." A mind stayed on Him is a mind at rest and at peace.

CHAPTER

9

Oh, Where Has
My Mind Run
Off to *This* Time?

n the previous chapter, we learned that a "too-busy" mind is not
normal. But mind-abnormality has more than one face. In this
chapter, you'll meet two more.

How many times has this happened to you? You're sitting in a
class at school, and, for a while, you are tuned in to everything the
instructor is saying. You're absorbing the information, even taking
notes. Then, for some reason, your mind decides to take a little

trip. Maybe to a friend's house, the mall, or across the country to visit a cousin.

After a while, the lecture starts coming through again, but you look at your watch and realize that, mentally speaking, you were somewhere else for the past twelve minutes.

This has happened to me, too, even at church. It's something common to all of us—it's average. But, it's not *normal*.

Too many people spend years allowing their minds to wander off. That's because they've never applied the principles of discipline to their thought life. They would never let a child, a younger sibling, or even a pet wander off to who-knows-where, but they do it with their thoughts all the time. After a while, it becomes almost like a habit.

Quite often, people who can't seem to concentrate think they are mentally deficient. But more than likely, it's just a lack of discipline that's at fault. After years of letting the mind gallop off to do what it wants to, it's hard to rein it back in.

Depriving yourself of proper nutrition can also weaken concentration. In particular, B-vitamins enhance the ability to concentrate. So, if you are plagued by an inability to focus, it might be worth a trip to a doctor or nutritionist.

Another big factor associated with poor concentration is fatigue. Have you ever lost track of time playing games, text-messaging, or chatting on-line late on a school night, then found it was virtually impossible to pay attention in class the next day?

I have found that when I get overtired, Satan will try to attack my mind, because he knows it's more difficult for me to resist him when I'm worn down.

Your mind can wander when you read, too. I can read a chapter in the Bible, get to the end, then realize that I don't have a shred of recollection about what I just read. I go back and read the chapter again, and it all seems new to me. This is because even though my eyes were scanning the words on the pages, my mind had gone somewhere else. It wasn't alert and available to process what I was reading. Because I failed to focus, I failed to comprehend.

In the book of Ecclesiastes, the wise man Solomon advises people to "give your mind to what you are doing" (5:1 AMP). Think about that advice. It means to commit your mind to the words on the page, the words in the song, the words in the sermon. This is what a speaker means when she says, "Give me your *full* attention."

The full attention thing has not been easy for me. I used to have a wandering mind, and I had to train it by discipline. The training was not easy, and I confess that I still have relapses. In defining the word *wander*, the dictionary uses words like, "move about aimlessly" and "amble." I can be writing a book and suddenly realize that I'm thinking about something that has nothing to do with the book or its topic.

I have definitely not arrived at some place of perfect concentration, but at least now I understand how important it is to guard my mind from ambling wherever it wishes, whenever it desires. And I'm aware of my tendency, so I'm more on-guard about it.

Simply being aware can make a big difference. In conversations with my husband, Dave, I used to listen for a while, then take a little mental vacation and miss huge chunks of what he was saying. There was a time when I would try to cover up my inattentiveness, nod affirmatively, and pretend I caught every single word. This was disrespectful, as well as dishonest.

Now, when this happens—and I admit that it still does once in a while—I stop Dave and say, "Can you repeat what you just said? I'm sorry, but I let my mind wander off, and I missed it."

It can be embarrassing to admit that you spaced out, but in the end it's much more respectful to someone than to have faked hearing. And, you won't have to miss out on a key piece of information or suffer the deeper embarrassment when asked a question like, "Do you agree with what I just said?" or "How does that plan sound to you?"

Being honest like this also shows people that you recognize you have a tendency and you're confronting it and working on it. And confronting problems is the only way to defeat them!

Another way to battle a wandering mind is to find ways to reinforce the messages God is trying to communicate to you. Many churches, for example, make CDs or cassette tapes of sermons available. Listening to these on the way to school or work, or while running errands, is a great way to emphasize key points or catch something you might have missed at church. A few churches even provide recent sermons on streaming audio, via their Web sites.

If you are studying a book of the Bible, try reading passages in a couple of different versions of the Bible. I've used this technique in this book. Sometimes, the different ways of phrasing a concept broaden and deepen our understanding of it.

Music is another great way to ward off a wandering mind. The rhythm, rhymes, and beat of a song can help you remember a Bible verse or key biblical truth.

A Wondering Mind

Before we conclude this chapter, it's time to meet Wandering Mind's cousin, Wondering Mind. And I should point out that I'm not talking about the kind of awe-filled wonder we feel toward God and His creation. This is wonder of another sort . . .

"I wonder what kind of grades I'll get this semester."

"I wonder if I'll get a good job someday."

"I wonder how old I'll live to be."

"I wonder how old I'll be when my hair turns gray—or starts to fall out."

Have you ever pondered thoughts like these? For me, my "wonders" are things like, "I wonder how my son is handling the pressure at his work," or "I wonder how many people will show up at the seminar I'm teaching—and I wonder what I should wear."

These kinds of statements reflect the kind of wonder that's defined as "a feeling of puzzlement or doubt."

If your mind is in a constant state of this kind of wonder, that's not normal. It's just a waste of time, and it stirs up unnecessary worry. I have found that I am much better off doing something positive, rather than just *wondering* about things all of the time.

For example, instead of wondering how my son is doing, I can pray for him, encourage him, and help him if he needs it. And instead of fretting over seminar attendance, I can prepare well, commit to doing my best, then turn the matter over to the Lord and trust Him to work out all things for good, regardless of who or how many show up.

The "puzzlement" brand of wondering breeds indecision, and indecision causes confusion. And this state of mind prevents us from receiving from God, by faith, His answers and direction for our lives.

Note that in Mark 11:23-24, Jesus does not say, "Whatever you ask for in prayer, wonder if you will get it." Instead, He says, "Whatever you ask for in prayer, *believe* that you will receive it!"

As Christians, we are sometimes called believers, not wandering wonderers. That's because we are supposed to believe, not doubt!

PART THREE

Six States You Do *Not* Want to Live In

INTRODUCTION

Think for a few minutes of the state you live in. What do you love about it? The weather? The beaches? The mountains? The food? The people? The recreational possibilities?

Now, what do you dislike about your state? The pollution? The crime? The traffic? Is there someplace else you'd rather live?

Well, no matter how you feel about the geographical state in which you reside, it's better than some of the states—the mental states—that we'll talk about in this section.

How Well Do You Know Your State?

This section of the book is about mental states, but let's not leave out the geographical states. Take a look at the two lists of ten states below. These states are national leaders in two important categories. Can you guess what they are?

List 1
1. Rhode Island
2. North Dakota
3. Wisconsin

4. South Dakota
5. Montana
6. Minnesota
7. Nebraska
8. Wyoming
9. Vermont
10. New Hampshire

[Answer: These are the top ten states for binge-drinking among eighteen- to twenty-five-year-olds—based on self-reports of binge-drinking in the previous 30 days![1]]

List 2

1. Rhode Island
2. Colorado
3. New Hampshire
4. New Mexico
5. Vermont
6. Arizona
7. Alaska
8. Maine
9. Massachusetts
10. Wyoming

[Answer: These are the top ten states for cocaine use among eighteen- to twenty-five-year-olds in the past year.[2]]

The State of Confusion

If any of you lacks wisdom, he should ask God, who gives
generously to all without finding fault, and it will be given to him.
But when he asks, he must believe and not doubt, because he who
doubts is like a wave of the sea, blown and tossed by the wind.
That man should not think he will receive anything from the Lord;
he is a double-minded man, unstable in all he does.
—James 1:5-8

D id you know that God is eager to give you wisdom—and that all you have to do is ask? It seems like a very simple deal: 1. You need wisdom and guidance about life. 2. You ask God for help. 3. God gives you what you need.

But many people make this simple three-step process needlessly complicated and ineffective.

Some of them ask God for wisdom, but, meanwhile, they are already busy trying to figure things out on their own. Others pray to become wiser, but their prayers are halfhearted and double-minded—along the lines of "God, I really need Your wisdom to help me make some good decisions about my friendships. But, on the other hand, You probably have more important prayers to answer than mine. Who knows if You're even hearing me now? Besides, I can't imagine myself ever being wise. That's not who I am. I always mess up, always make bad choices. I don't even know why I'm bothering to pray."

Does this kind of prayer sound familiar to you? Have you ever started a prayer by sincerely seeking God's guidance, then gradually seen your prayer morph into a weak list of doubts and insecurities?

Read the end of the Scripture passage that kicked off this section again. The Amplified Version of the Bible translates "double-minded man" as "a man of two minds." Sounds like a horror movie, doesn't it: "The Man with Two Minds." And, indeed it is horrible to live with a mind that wants to go in two opposite directions at once.

I know the horrors. I lived much of my life as "The Meyer with Two Minds." I didn't realize that the devil had declared war against me, and my mind was the battlefield. I was totally confused about everything, and I didn't know why.

A Reasonable Proposal

One thing that added to my confusion was too much reasoning. Yes, you read that right. Of course, reasoning is often a good thing, but not always. You might be skeptical about this position, but stay with me here. I have good reasons for warning you about an over-reliance on reasoning—and I think you'll find them reasonable.

Reasoning occurs when a person begins to ask the "why" questions about something. Now, this is a good thing with questions like, "Why did the smoke alarm just go off?" or "Why is my car engine making that weird noise?"

However, in other situations, Satan can use your own reasoning power against you. The Lord may be guiding you, inspiring you to do something, but because it doesn't make sense or seem logical, you might disregard His prompting. The Bible warns us that when we are not open to God's Spirit, the things of God seem like foolishness to us (1 Corinthians 2:14).

Here's an example that might help you understand this principle. If you're like most teens, you've probably seen at least some of the movie *The Karate Kid*. Remember when Mr. Miyagi first started to teach his young pupil, Daniel, about the martial arts? He didn't take him to a karate school and show him punches and kicks. Instead, he had him paint a fence, sand a floor, and wax a car.

Daniel, understandably, was furious. He *reasoned*, "This makes no sense to me. I want to learn karate, not do a bunch of chores. Maybe this old Miyagi dude is just using me to get me to do his work for him."

The reality was that the chores Miyagi had chosen for Daniel were exactly what he needed to build the strength, form, and discipline to become a champion fighter. But if Daniel would have trusted his reasoning powers, rather than his teacher, he would have never become the skilled karate kid he hoped to be.

Or, you might have heard the story of the little boy trapped near a second-story window of a burning house. His father stood below the window, begging his child to jump. But the boy, because he couldn't see his father due to all the smoke, didn't want to jump. It was not reasonable for him to jump to someone he couldn't even see. It wasn't until the boy trusted his father more than his own judgment that he was able to leap to safety.

Learning to understand how to balance the reasoning of the

mind with the obedience of the Spirit can impact your life in ways big and small.

For example, one morning as I was getting dressed to minister in a weekly meeting, I started thinking about a woman who ran the ministry of helps connected to the meetings. She had always been so faithful about her duties, and I felt a desire bloom in my heart: I wanted to do something that would bless her.

"Father," I prayed, "Ruth Ann has been such a blessing to us all these years. What can I do to bless her?"

Immediately, my eyes fell on a new red dress hanging in my closet, and I felt in my heart the Lord's urging to give that dress to Ruth Ann.

First, a couple of things about this red dress: 1. I purchased it three months previously but never wore it. It was still hanging inside the plastic bag I'd brought it home in. 2. I really liked the dress, but every time I had thought about wearing it, I ultimately decided on something else.

It should have been a no-brainer to give this dress to Ruth Ann, right?

Wrong. My double-minded thinking hijacked my God-inspired idea. Instead of simply blessing Ruth Ann with a gift that God had conveniently placed right in front of my face, I started to reason . . .

I haven't even had the chance to wear the dress even once, and I really like it.

The dress was rather expensive. Shouldn't I get some wear out of this investment before just giving it away?

I bought red and silver earrings just to match the dress.

In the end, I reasoned myself right out of doing something kind for a deserving person. It took very little time, and within a few minutes, I forgot about the whole thing and went on about my business.

Weeks later, I was getting ready for another meeting at the same location as the one before. Again, Ruth Ann's name was impressed upon my heart. I began to pray almost the same prayer as before, asking God how I could bless Ruth Ann. I finished praying and saw the dress again. I felt weighed down by guilt. I remembered the previous incident, troubled at how quickly it had slipped my mind the first time around.

This time, there would be no rationalizing my way out of things. I had to face the fact that God was showing me what to do. I needed to either do it, or just be blunt and say, "I know what You are showing me, Lord, but I am just not going to do it." And I love the Lord too much to willfully, knowingly disobey Him.

As I prayed about the situation, I realized that the Bible doesn't say we can give away only our old, unwanted stuff. Sure, it would be more of a sacrifice to give an expensive new dress away, but that would mean the gift would be more of a blessing to Ruth Ann. God showed me that, in reality, I had bought the dress for Ruth Ann. That was the reason I could never bring myself to wear it. The Lord had intended all along to use me as His agent to show kindness to Ruth Ann. But I had clung to my own ideas, until I was finally willing to lay down my ideas and be led by God's Spirit.

I have found that God wants me to obey Him, whether or not I feel like it, or whether or not I think it's a good idea. When God speaks, He wants me to mobilize, not rationalize.

By the way, you might be wondering if I finally gave Ruth Ann the dress. Yes, I did. And she now works in our office full-time and occasionally wears the dress to work. She looks great in it.

Who Are You Gonna Lean On?

Lean on, trust in, and be confident in the Lord with all your heart and mind and do not rely on your own insight or understanding.
—Proverbs 3:5 AMP

It's significant that this verse from Proverbs mentions both the heart and the mind. The mind and the spirit can and do work together to help people follow God. You're using your mind to read these words right now, and, at the same time (I hope), the book is touching your heart—your spirit—as well.

Problems occur when people elevate their minds above their spirits. The spirit is the more noble of the two and should always be honored above the mind.

For example, let's say that you're facing a tough final exam in one of your classes. A fellow student hacks into the school's database, scores the answer key, and emails it to everyone in the class. Your spirit tells you that it would be wrong to cheat. In your spirit, in your gut, you feel the magnetic pull to action, to do the right thing.

But, let's see what happens if you start second-guessing and rationalizing . . .

"If everyone has the answers, it's really not cheating. Cheating is when you have an unfair advantage over other students. That's not the case here."

"I really need a good test grade in this class. It will help my GPA, which will help me get a scholarship, which will make me less of a financial drain on my parents."

"The teacher is lousy. I hate her style—it makes it hard for me to learn. I deserve some kind of advantage here."

"If I'm the only one who doesn't cheat, it's not fair to me. Why should I be the only one to suffer?"

"I'm a decent student. If I don't cheat—and then get the low-est grade in the class—the teacher will be suspicious. I could get everyone else in trouble. I almost have to cheat, or there's gonna be a big blow-up."

Do you see what can happen if we allow reasoning to detour us from following what God has impressed on our hearts? Do you see the kind of mental gymnastics we can put ourselves through?

I don't know about you, but I want God to reveal things to me in such a way that I know in my spirit what I should do. I don't want to mentally run around and around an issue or problem until I am dizzy and exhausted. I want to experience the peace of mind and heart that comes from trusting God, not my own un-derstanding.

You and I need to progress in our spiritual journey until we reach the place where we are satisfied to know the One Who Knows, even if we ourselves don't know.

The States of Doubt and Unbelief

A t first glance, it might seem like these "states" are redundantly named. Aren't doubt and unbelief pretty much the same thing?

The two are related, and both are dangerous places where Satan would love to drag you. Let's look at both doubt and unbelief, so that you can know exactly which one you're being lured or pushed toward.

The Dirt on Doubt

A great reference tool, Vine's *An Expository Dictionary of New Testament Words*, notes that to doubt is "to stand in two ways . . . implying uncertainty which way to take, . . . said of believers whose faith is small . . . being anxious, through a distracted state of mind, of wavering between hope and fear."[1]

Here's a story that brings the definition to life:

A sick man wanted to be healed. So, he prayed and quoted scriptures about healing. He believed that he would be healed. But all the while, doubts invaded his mind. This tension made him grow discouraged.

Then God allowed him a glimpse of the spiritual world. This is what the man saw: A demon was hurling lies at him, telling him, "You're not going to get healed; all of this reciting Bible verses like some kind of magic words—that's not going to work!"

But the man also saw that each time he proclaimed God's Word, a light would come out of his mouth, like a sword, and force the demon to cower and tumble backward.

This vision made a profound impression on the man. He understood that it was important to keep speaking God's Word, because it was having an effect. And the very fact that it was effective was prompting the demon to use doubt to get the man to stop. Doubt is a tool of the enemy; it's not something from God.

The Bible promises that God gives everyone a measure of faith (Romans 12:3). He puts faith in our hearts, and the devil tries to negate that faith by attacking us with doubt. This is why it's so important to know and understand the Bible—to memorize key verses and be able to look up passages that build our faith. If we understand God's Word, we will recognize when the devil is trying to plant lies in our minds.

Uncovering Unbelief

While doubt is belief tinged with second-guessing and uncertainty, *unbelief* is a lack of belief or faith. Unbelief can even grow into an all-out rejection of faith. Unbelief is a dangerous state to stumble into, but it can be avoided.

Remember the story about Abraham—how God promised this 100-year-old man (with an almost equally old wife) that he would be the forefather of many nations? Abraham heard God's promise and didn't weaken in his faith—even though a spirit of unbelief attacked him like a swarm of angry bees.

As Abraham stood up to the temptation to disbelieve God's promise, the Bible tells us that he grew stronger in his faith; he felt increasingly empowered by it. This is a key point. You see, when God tells or asks us to do something, He also provides the faith and courage for us to follow through. He doesn't send you into a battle with no weapons or defense, shrugging His shoulders and saying, "Dude, I wouldn't go into battle unprepared like you are! Good luck, though. Let me know how things turn out."

Instead, God gives us the ability to believe we can do what needs doing. And He'll help us get stronger as we turn to Him and His Word for wisdom and power. This makes Satan freak out. He knows how dangerous a person with a heart full of faith can be. That's why he does everything he can to weaken our faith. That's why he lies in an attempt to get us to stop believing. And these lies can be compelling.

Let me give you an example, from the time that I received my calling from God to go into ministry. It was an ordinary morning for me, except that, three weeks previously, I had been filled with the Holy Spirit and was hungry to grow in my faith. I was listening to a teaching tape by a minister named Ray Mossholder. The tape was titled "Cross Over to the Other Side." As I listened to the tape, my heart stirred, and I was amazed that someone could talk about just one Scripture passage for a whole hour—and be interesting the entire time.

Later, as I made my bed, I suddenly felt an intense desire well up in me: I wanted to teach God's Word. Next, I heard the Lord communicating something to me: "You will go all over the place and teach My Word, and you will have a large teaching-tape ministry."

If you had known me at the time, you would have agreed with me that there was no logical reason to believe this urging was really from God—or that I would be up to the task. I had a lot of problems. I did not appear to be "ministry material." But the Bible says that God can take what people might think is weak and foolish (1 Corinthians 1:27) and use it to confound even the wise. And He looks at our hearts, not our outward appearance (1 Samuel 16:7).

So, although there was nothing about the surface, "natural" Joyce Meyer to indicate I should believe God's vision for my life and the desire He planted in me, I relied on promises like those in 1 Corinthians and 1 Samuel, and I was filled with faith that I could do what the Lord wanted me to do. I resisted the temptation to disbelieve God's guidance. When God calls, He gives you the desire, faith, and ability to answer the call.

I responded to my call by investing years of study and training, waiting for the right moment to begin my ministry. And during this time, the devil regularly attacked me with both doubt and unbelief. God's vision for me was planted like a seed in my heart, just like you'd plant a seed in a garden. While the seed is germinating and growing beneath the surface, Satan works hard to get you to dig it up. He'll tell you it will never grow, or that if it does, it will become a puny and sickly plant that will embarrass you— so you might as well dig it up, or at least ignore it and not bother to nurture and water it.

If You Wanna Walk on Water, Get Out of the Boat!

If you attended Sunday school as a kid, you probably remember this story: Jesus' disciples are out in a boat, a long way from land, when they get caught in a violent storm. The wind and the sea are kicking their boat around like a hackey-sack.

Then, at somewhere between 3:00 and 6:00 in the morning, Jesus approaches them, walking on top of the sea. Being tough, sea-worthy dudes, the disciples start screaming like a bunch of wimps. They think Jesus is some kind of sea-ghost, come to terrorize them.

Jesus shouts over the screaming, "Take courage. It is I. Don't be afraid."

Peter, perhaps the most impulsive of all the disciples, shouts back, "Lord, if it's You, tell me to come to You on the water."

Jesus gives permission, and Peter clambers out of the boat and, to his amazement, begins to walk on the water toward Jesus. But then he starts to panic in the strong wind and churning sea. He starts to sink; he thinks he's going to drown.

But Jesus shoots His hand toward Peter. He grabs Peter's hand and holds him up. "You of little faith," He says, "why did you doubt?"

Then Peter and Jesus get into the boat. As they do, the sea calms—as do Peter's frazzled nerves!

We can learn a lot from this incident. It took faith for Peter to get out of the boat. Notice that none of the other disciples wanted to try this new extreme sport, Early Morning Whitewater Walking.

But then Peter made a mistake. He started to focus on the storm around him rather than the Savior right in front of him. Doubt and unbelief pressed in on him, and he wiped out like a novice surfboarder trying to ride a half-pipe.

When storms come into your life, be strong. Trust in God's promises and His everlasting love for you. The devil brings storms into your life to intimidate and scare you. He wants you to focus on the circumstances, the "facts"—not God's vision for your life, a vision that is bigger than any circumstance!

Here's an example that will illustrate the point: A friend of mine was confused when he graduated from Bible college. God had placed a desire in his heart to start a church in St. Louis, Missouri. However, as he considered his calling, he also took note of the fact that he had a wife, a child, and another kid on the way. And his entire budget to start his church was the approximately fifty bucks in his pocket.

The circumstances didn't seem to be leading him to a church. Meanwhile, he received attractive job offers to join the staffs of two large, well-established ministries. The salaries were right, and the ministry opportunities were many and enticing. Beyond these factors, he knew it would be an honor and a great résumé-builder to be a part of either ministry.

My friend deliberated over his three job options, and the more he pondered them, the more confused he became. His mind was assaulted with doubt. Right after graduation, he had known in his heart exactly what he should do, but now he found himself wavering. His life and financial circumstances didn't favor following his original plan. The two offers were tempting. What was the right thing to do?

He decided to ask a pastor from one of the ministries for advice. This wise man told him, "Go somewhere, get quiet and still, and turn your head off. Look into your heart; see what's there, and do it!"

Following the pastor's advice, my friend quickly sensed that his heart was in St. Louis and the church he wanted to start there. He had no clue how he would build a church with only fifty bucks to start with, but he moved forward, obeying God's call.

Today, my friend is founder and senior pastor of a large church and has a worldwide outreach, as well. Thousands of lives have been blessed and transformed through this church. I served as an associate pastor there for five years, and my Life in the Word ministry was born during my time working with this friend.

It is truly marvelous to see what happens when we follow God and guard the borders of our minds against incursions from doubt and unbelief.

God has a great plan for your life. Don't let the devil hijack your life. Don't let him steal from you the peace and fulfillment God wants you to enjoy. To achieve this goal, you're gonna have to kick some tail. That's right; you heard me.

Second Corinthians 10:4-5 says, "The weapons we fight with . . . have divine power to demolish strongholds. We demolish arguments and every pretension that sets itself up against the knowledge of God, and we take captive every thought and make it obedient to Christ."

Note the words in this passage. You are supposed to demolish the devil's arguments and pretension. You don't leave one brick standing on another. And no random thought escapes in this battle. You take every one, and make it obedient to Christ.

This all might sound extreme, but remember, this is war, and you don't fight a war halfway.

The State of Worry

Maybe you've learned how to defeat the enemies of doubt and unbelief, the subjects of the previous chapter. But that doesn't mean the battle for your mind is over. Satan has other dangerous places he can take you. This chapter will focus on one rather subtly dangerous one—worry.

You've heard of people being addicted to alcohol, cigarettes, meth, gambling, food, sex, and a host of other things. But did you know you can be addicted to worry? That's right; there are people who are addicted to worrying over their lives, and when they can't find their own stuff to worry about, they'll start worrying about their friends, relatives, and neighbors. How do I know this? I was addicted to worry myself, so I am well-qualified to describe this condition.

At one time in my life, I worried *constantly*. There was always something troubling me. As a result, I never enjoyed the peace that Jesus died for me to have. It's impossible to worry and live in peace at the same time. Think about it: *Worry* is defined as feeling uneasy, troubled, anxious, or distressed. Worry can also mean being plagued by nagging concerns. I have also heard worrying described as tormenting oneself with disturbing thoughts.

That last definition was key for me. It helped me decide, forcefully, that I am too smart to torment *myself*. I believe every Christian is too smart to fall into this trap. We just need to realize that worry never makes anything better. Never. So, why waste time worrying?

It's the time-wasting, energy-draining properties of worry that make it such an effective satanic weapon. If the devil can keep your mind preoccupied with worries, you won't be using your mind in productive, God-honoring ways.

Jesus warned against this kind of worry. In Matthew 6:25–27, He instructs, "Therefore I tell you, do not worry about your life, what you will eat or drink; or about your body, what you will wear. Is not life more important than food, and the body more important than clothes? Look at the birds of the air; they do not sow or reap or store away in barns, and yet your heavenly Father feeds them. Are you not much more valuable than they? Who of you by worrying can add a single hour to his life?"

It might do us all some good to do some bird-watching every now and then, as the Lord instructed. We should note how well our feathered friends are cared for. They don't have a clue where their next meal is coming from—or when they'll get it. And yet, I've never seen a St. Louis cardinal (the bird, not the baseball player) sitting on a tree branch and having a nervous breakdown due to worry.

I know that some teens struggle with low self-image, but surely you can believe that you're more valuable than a bird, right? And look at how well God takes care of them. What's more, our heavenly Father delights—yes, delights—in giving His children good things. But we won't be able to receive and enjoy these things if we are occupied by worry. If we focus on worrying about tomorrow, we can't live and celebrate today.

Author Max Lucado titled one of his books *Grace for the Moment*. It's a good title, because that's how God's grace works in our lives. God's grace is always on hand to help us handle whatever we're dealing with *now*, at this moment. His grace for tomorrow will arrive tomorrow—when we need it.

We've seen that worry is a bad state to be in, but what about our counter-weapons to avoiding it? Here are a few great ones:

1. <u>Speaking the Word.</u> I highly recommend speaking God's Word out loud, when worry encroaches on your territory. You might feel like this isn't your personal spiritual style, or you might feel weird reciting or reading a Scripture passage out loud. But try it. After all, the Bible is described as a sword, and, during an attack, a sword won't do you any good in its sheath. For example, you might want to encourage yourself with the words of 1 Peter 5:7, "Casting the whole of your care [all your anxieties, all your worries, all your concerns, once and for all] on Him, for He cares for you affectionately and cares about you watchfully." There are two words you might want to say with extra emphasis:

Affectionately—God's care for you shines with genuine love for you. He doesn't care for you out of duty or obligation. He likes you; He loves you.

Watchfully—God is diligent as He watches over you. He doesn't doze off or get distracted if a bunch of angels get too loud playing volleyball. His loving eyes follow you wherever you go.

2. <u>Toss Worries to God.</u> Satan will try to hand you lots of worries and stress; fortunately, you are under no obligation to hang on to them. Remember the verse about "casting anxieties" on God? When you read that, you might have thought of "casting" in the sense of laying something at God's feet. That's a nice image, but it's not what the Bible means here. In this case, to cast worries means to hurl them like fastballs. Don't hang on to worries. Don't even say, "Next time I go to church or youth group, I'm going to hand these worries off to God. Maybe symbolically lay them in front of the sanctuary." Don't wait: Pick 'em up and fire 'em God's way. Believe me; He can catch them, and He knows what to do with them.

3. <u>Rest in God.</u> Two artists were asked to paint pictures of peace. One painted a serene nature scene, with a still lake as its focal point. The other painted a tree branch extended over a raging, rushing waterfall. Perched in the branch was a bird in its nest, resting in the security of its home. The bird seemed to understand that in its nest, it was safe from the danger below.

Which picture represents peace and rest? The second one. Think about it. The first picture is static, stagnant. The second one truly depicts peace, because there can be no peace without opposition. God won't remove all opposition from your life, but He can give you a sense of rest and peace in the midst of life's storms. So, rest in God's love and His plan for your life. He will meet your needs.

The State of Judgment

I knew a woman married to a wealthy businessman. This man was rather quiet, and his wife wanted him to be more outgoing. He was knowledgeable about many topics, and his wife got angry when they were out with friends and he wouldn't contribute anything to the conversation—even when the topic was something he knew thoroughly.

One evening, after the couple returned from a party, the woman tore into him. "Why didn't you speak up tonight? You just sat there like a dummy! Our friends are going to think you're stupid or uninformed! You acted as if you didn't know anything at all!"

The husband responded, "I already know what *I* know. I try to be quiet and listen so I can find out what others know."

I think this attitude is why the guy is wealthy; he's wise, and few people gain wealth without wisdom. This man was willing to sit and listen to what other people knew, what they thought, without passing judgment on them or criticizing their position on an issue.

I used to be a critical person. I always seemed to be able to see what was wrong with something or someone—instead of what was right. Some personality types are simply more given to finding fault than others. Those who tend to be controlling often see what's wrong with something first, and they are quite generous in sharing their critiques with others.

I needed to realize, as we all do, that everyone is different. What might be the right course of action for me might not be right for my friend. I'm not talking about universal things like "Love the Lord your God" here, but rather the thousands of personal choices that people make every day. People have a right to make these choices without outside interference.

For example, my husband and I differ on our approach to a lot of stuff, such as how to decorate a house. If we go shopping for household items together, it seems like Dave always likes one thing, while I like something different. Why? Simply because we are two different people. His opinion is as good as mine, and vice versa.

This seems like an easy concept, but it took me years to understand that Dave didn't have something wrong with him just because he didn't agree with me on everything. And I wasn't shy about sharing just how wrong I thought he was. My attitude created a lot of friction between us, and it hurt our relationship.

Judgment and criticism like this are the fruit of a deeper problem: pride. The Bible repeatedly warns against getting too high-minded and having a too-high opinion of ourselves. If we are prideful, we tend to look down on others and value them as less than ourselves. Simply put, the Lord detests this attitude.

Galatians 6:3 notes, "For if any person thinks himself to be somebody [too important to condescend to shoulder another's load] when he is nobody [of superiority except in his own estimation], he deceives and deludes and cheats himself" (AMP).

Suppose one of your neighbors comes to your door and says, "You know, I really don't like the way you look. You should dress differently and do something else with your hair. Your look just isn't working for me. And while you're at it, find some cooler friends. The people you hang around with are a bunch of losers. One final thing: Your house is ugly, too."

How would you respond? Have you ever been judged like this? Ever done any judging yourself?

I did. I used to entertain myself by sitting in the park or the mall and watching people go by, forming opinions about them—their clothing, hairstyles, companions, and so on. Now, we can't always prevent ourselves from having opinions, but we don't have to express them and hurt others. We don't have to dwell on the opinions until they become judgments.

Also, I believe that we can grow and mature to the point where we don't find ourselves formulating so many negative opinions of the people around us. We can control more and more of this portion of the battlefields of our minds.

I frequently find myself saying, "Joyce, it's none of your business."

One great way to fight your way out of the state of judgment is to rely on the great counter-weapon to judgment: love.

You and I have the ability to love others—and the command from God to use that ability. If we live a life of love, we protect ourselves from falling into being judgmental and prideful.

Proverbs 16:24 says "Pleasant words are as a honeycomb, sweet to the mind and healing to the body" (AMP).

We all make mistakes, and we all have weaknesses. But instead of having a hard-hearted, critical mind-set toward others, the Bible instructs us to forgive one another, to show mercy, and to speak words of love and encouragement.

You'll find that if you focus on finding what's good in others and speaking "pleasant words," you won't have the time or inclination to judge them. And you'll find that as your attitude changes, your joy increases.

Jesus wants you to enjoy life. Judgment and criticism never bring joy. Showing love does. The choice is yours.

The State of Passivity

ave you ever been told, "You need to study/exercise/go to church/clean your room," only to respond, "But I don't feel like it!"?

Many people, even those who believe in God, are so passive in their approach to life that a mere absence of feeling is all it takes to stop them from doing what they should do. They attend church when they feel like it. They praise God only when their emotions are charged up. They donate time or money only when they're feeling generous.

Ephesians 4:27 (KJV) warns, "Neither give place to the devil," but many people don't realize a vital truth: Empty space is a place. In other words, a passive mind is like an unguarded fortress. The enemy can easily overrun it. To win the battle for your mind, Satan doesn't necessarily need your mind to be corrupted and filled with impure thoughts, motives, and lies. An unoccupied, lazy mind will do just fine.

For example, a person might tell himself, *I'm doing pretty well. I don't think bad thoughts about others, and I don't go around criticizing them either. I just keep to myself.*

The problem with this thinking is that there are aggressive sins, sins of commission, and there are passive sins, sins of omission. Harsh, hateful words have ravaged many relationships, but marriages and friendships have also been destroyed by cold silence, by kind, healing words that were never uttered.

Pulverizing Passivity

Years ago, my husband had a passivity problem. He was an active person in some phases of his life. He went to work every day and played golf on Saturdays. (He was also, as I've mentioned before, a disciplined Sunday-afternoon sports watcher.)

But beyond these activities, Dave lacked motivation. If I needed a picture hung on a wall, it might take him three or four weeks to get around to it. This passivity created a lot of tension between us. It seemed to me that he did only what he wanted to do, and nothing beyond that.

Dave loved the Lord and sought divine guidance for his

problem. God revealed to him that his passivity was part of Satan's battle plan. In some areas of his life, Dave had relinquished territory to the enemy.

Dave was also passive when it came to studying the Bible and praying. I was aware of this weakness, so it was hard for me to listen to him and respect his opinion. I had a problem with rebellion anyway, so you can imagine how the devil used our weaknesses against us. Dave would tell me that I was always running ten miles ahead of God. I countered that he was ten miles behind. A lot of people get divorced over problems like the one(s) we had.

Fortunately, God's Spirit revealed to Dave how the enemy was oppressing him through his passivity. Dave determined in his heart and mind that he would once again become a more active person in all areas of his life.

He began to wake up at 5 in the morning to read the Bible and pray before he went to work. The battle was on, and it was not easy. Satan did not want to give up the battleground he had conquered, so he did what he could to break Dave's will. Sometimes, Dave would wake up but then fall asleep on the couch a while later. But even on these mornings when fatigue got the better of him, Dave knew he was making progress—simply because he made the effort to get out of bed and strengthen his spiritual life.

On some mornings, Dave stayed awake but got bored with his studying—or couldn't understand a particular scripture. At other times, he wondered if his prayers were getting through. But he remembered what the Holy Spirit had revealed to him about his passivity and kept striving for progress.

Eventually, I began to notice that when I needed Dave to hang a picture or fix something around the house, he responded immediately. He became more decisive. The new discipline in his spiritual life was manifesting itself in other areas.

I must be honest and tell you that the change from passive to active was not easy for Dave. It took a matter of months, not days or weeks to overcome.

But my husband persisted, and now he is not passive at all. He is the administrator for the Joyce Meyer Ministries, overseeing all of the radio and television outreach. He also bears full financial responsibility for the ministry. He travels full-time with me and makes the decisions about our travel schedule.

He is also an excellent family man. He still plays golf and watches sports sometimes, but he does the other things he is supposed to do, as well. Knowing him now and seeing all that he accomplishes, no one would ever think he was once plagued by passivity.

What Dave learned is that right actions follow right thinking. It's impossible to get from wrong behavior to right behavior without first changing your thoughts. A passive person might genuinely want to do the right thing, but he will never do it until he activates his mind and disciplines it to focus on God's Word and God's will.

For example, a man at one of my seminars came to us and shared a problem: He was a prisoner of lust. He loved his wife and didn't want their marriage to be destroyed, but he couldn't keep his eyes—or his hands—off of other women. "Joyce," he said, "I just cannot seem to stay away from other women. Will you pray for my deliverance? I have been prayed for many times, but I never seem to make any progress."

Here's what God's Spirit prompted me to tell him: "Yes, I will pray for you, but you must be accountable for what you are allowing to play on the movie screen of your mind. You cannot visualize pornographic pictures in your head—or imagine yourself with these other women—if you ever want to enjoy freedom."

You can't entertain wrong or impure thoughts in your head and experience a freeing breakthrough in your life. Your mind cannot be a playground for sin. Jesus makes this point well in Matthew 5:27-28: "You have heard that it was said, 'Do not commit adultery.' But I tell you that anyone who looks at a woman lustfully has already committed adultery with her in his heart."

If you have a tendency toward passivity, take the initiative. Take action. Don't just wish that things will get better on their own, or as you mature. Make decisions. Make commitments. Plan to avoid sin.

If you want to enjoy the good life God has planned for you, keep your mind focused on good things. Don't let damaging thoughts creep into your head, and don't play with them if they do sneak in.

If you truly desire victory over your problems, you must have a *backbone*, not a *wishbone*. Be active, not passive. You will act right as you think right. Don't be passive in your mind. Start choosing right thoughts, right now!

PART FOUR

Unheavenly
Head-Spaces

INTRODUCTION

Now that our tour of some undesirable "states" is complete, it's time to go further, to visit the "cities"—the specific attitudes—within those mental states.

If your head is in any of the places I'll describe in this section, it will negatively affect your inner life and your outer circumstances. You can even be on your way to the "Promised Land" and not enjoy the journey if your mind isn't right.

For example, I can recall a time when my circumstances were really pretty good. Dave and I had a nice home, three lovely children, good jobs, and enough money to live comfortably.

But I could not enjoy our blessings because of some damaging mind-sets that plagued me. My life seemed like a wilderness to me because of the way I perceived things. I was dying in the wilderness, but God in His mercy shined a light in my darkness and led me out.

I pray that this section will be a light to you, free you from unheavenly head-spaces, and prepare you to walk out of your wilderness and into God's glorious light.

UNHEAVENLY
HEAD-SPACE #1

"I don't wanna take responsibility for my spirituality—isn't that what we have pastors and parents for?"

During his time in junior high and high school, a teen guy attended a certain church camp every summer. The camp always ended with an emotional fireside service, in which people could share what was on their hearts, confess sin, ask for prayer, or praise God for something.

At his first fireside service, this guy approached the flames and tossed in a pack of Marlboros. He tearfully related how he had been addicted to the smokes and that by "casting them into the fire," he was demonstrating a rededication of his life to God.

The next summer, the same thing happened. The only difference was that the dude had changed cigarette brands over the course of the year.

Summer number three eventually rolled around, there was another fireside service, and . . . you guessed it. It got to become a sad joke among the other camp vets.

We shouldn't judge this guy, of course. It is easy to get emotional and full of good intentions when God first speaks to us and prompts us to do something—or stop doing something. And many of us don't finish what we start, once the emotion goes away and we realize there's more involved than goose bumps or a few tears.

Many new ventures, or "rededications," are exciting simply because they are new. And that excitement will help you burst out of the starting blocks, but it won't get you to the finish line. It takes perseverance and a sense of responsibility to finish what you start.

The teen in our story wasn't able to take responsibility for his actions. The camp counselors and speakers inspired him. They motivated him to make a decision. But it was his responsibility to stick by that decision, and that's where he faltered.

There was a time in your life when you had zero responsibility. Too bad you were too young to remember it. It was when you were first born. Every single need was attended to by someone else. But as you grew up, you were expected to take more and more responsibility. Right now, you might have a parent, sibling, teacher, or coach who does some things for you, but with other things, you're expected to take the lead.

It's the same scenario with God. He desires to teach His children responsibility. And the more spiritual gifts and opportunities He blesses you with, the more He wants you to do with them.

The Lord has given me an amazing opportunity to be in full-time ministry—to teach His Word on national TV and radio—to preach the Gospel all over the world—to write books that are read by millions. But I can assure you that there is a responsibility side to what I do, which many people know nothing about. A ministry like ours is not one big ongoing media event.

Many people apply for jobs with us, thinking it would be the greatest thing in the world to be associated with a high-profile Christian ministry. Later, some of them are dismayed to discover that they have to do work here, just like anyplace else. They have to wake up in the morning, get to work on time, attend to their daily tasks, and follow the leadership of their managers.

When people come to work with us, I tell them up front that we don't float around on a cloud all day, singing the "Hallelujah Chorus." We work. We work hard. We work with integrity, and we do what we do with excellence. Sure, it is a privilege to work as part of a ministry, but I emphasize with new employees that when the goose bumps have vanished, we'll still be present, expecting high levels of responsibility.

God expects the same thing. He wants you to keep living for Him even when the goose bumps are gone.

You will probably have a few people in your life to encourage you in your Christian life, but they won't always be right at your side. Like a champion distance runner, you're going to have to be able to push yourself when there's no one else present to pace you or shout encouragement into your ear or gush, "Great job!" at the end of every run.

All of us must become motivated from within. We must live our lives before God, knowing that He sees all and that our rewards will come from Him—if we are responsible to do what He wants us to do.

"My future is determined by my past and my present."

As you've read elsewhere in this book, I come from a background of abuse. I was raised in a dysfunctional home, and my childhood was filled with fear and torment. Maybe you can relate to this.

You've probably heard psychologists and counselors note that a child's personality is formed within the first five years of his or her life. As you can imagine, then, my personality was a mess! I had to put up a brave front to hide my fear. And I built walls of protection around myself to keep people from hurting me any more. I locked people out of my heart—and, as a result, I locked myself in.

Here's another way I coped with my fear and hurt: I became a controller. I believed that the only way I could survive in life was to be in control. If I could control relationships and circumstances, I reasoned, no one could hurt me again.

Does this sound like you, or someone you know?

As I became a young adult, I really tried to live for Christ, to follow His teachings. But I struggled. The cloud of my past hung over me, making it hard to face the future with optimism. I thought, *How could anyone with my kind of past really be all right as a person? It's impossible!*

As I read the Bible and prayed, though, I realized that Jesus said He would heal the sick, the brokenhearted, the wounded. I was trapped in a prison, but Jesus came to open the doors and set me free. His specialty was helping people just like me. He gave me a positive vision for my life. He led me to believe that my future wasn't determined by what had happened in the past—or what was going on in the present.

Like me, you might have endured a miserable past—and the circumstances you are in right now might give you little reason for hope. But I say to you, boldly, *Your future can be filled with joy, meaning, and peace.* I am living proof of this, and you can be, too.

So, adopt a new mind-set. Believe that with God all things are possible. Remember, He created the entire universe out of nothing! So, if you believe you are nothing, give your nothingness to Him and watch Him work! All it takes is faith. Believe, throw yourself into His loving arms, and He will do the rest.

Here's one of the coolest things that can happen when you allow God to turn a dim, bleak past into a bright shining future:

you can break the destructive patterns that have plagued your family relationships.

If you've had an unhealthy relationship with a parent or step-parent, you can say, "This stops with me." For instance, if you have been constantly criticized and ridiculed, you can resolve to speak words of hope and encouragement to the family members you have now—and the ones you will have someday. You can help create a legacy of light where there was once only darkness.

As you reverse these destructive patterns, giving to others the things you once craved, you will find that it's unbelievably healing to you.

"It's my way or the highway."

You might hear pastors and educators complaining, "Today's teens are more stubborn and rebellious than ever."

I suppose the question is up for debate, but throughout history, there have been many, many groups who could be strong contenders for the Most Stubborn title. For example, the Old Testament is filled with stories about the Israelites and their continued rebellion against God. So many times they defiantly turned their backs on God, then came whining to Him when they got in trouble. Next, they would obey for a while, until their circumstances improved and they forgot how miserable they were when they were living disobediently.

After a while, the Israelites would get cocky again, and the whole cycle would repeat itself. It's almost unbelievable that after experiencing great blessings and terrible punishments so many times that these people still wouldn't learn.

Maybe you can identify with the Israelites. You want to control your own life, and you're happy to obey God—as long as He doesn't cramp your style. I can empathize with you.

I believe I was born with a strong personality, and I was destined to become a "do-it-my-way" person, no matter what kind of upbringing I had. But the years I spent being abused and controlled just added fuel to my rebellious fire. I didn't trust people in authority; I resented them. I became a person who resisted correction, disobeyed rules, and was difficult to manage. My attitude was simple: Nobody is going to tell me what to do!

Obviously, God had to deal with my attitude before I could become an effective servant for Him. God can't shape clay that isn't moldable and pliable. I could not allow my past to become an excuse for resisting God's shaping of my life. To live the life of a winner, I had to show God prompt, exact obedience in all things.

As I worked toward this goal, I discovered that obedience is a process. As I laid aside my will and did God's will, I found my ability to obey was improving steadily.

It's important to continually improve our ability to obey, because God requires our obedience in all things. We shouldn't hold back any areas of our lives from Him. We can't close any doors to Him.

Here's why total obedience to God is so vital. Most scholars agree that King Solomon, a man to whom God gave more wisdom than anyone else, wrote the book of Ecclesiastes. Solomon was the Number One Wise Guy.

Unfortunately, Solomon made many tragic mistakes in his life and spent much of his time being miserable—despite being amazingly wealthy and powerful. Early in Ecclesiastes, he cries out, "Meaningless! Meaningless! Utterly meaningless! Everything is meaningless." (See Ecclesiastes 1:2.)

Later he goes on to list what he finds meaningless. Here is Solomon's Top-8 List of Meaningless Things:

1. Wisdom
2. Pleasure
3. Folly
4. Work
5. Advancement
6. Riches
7. Youth and Vigor
8. Everything (pretty much)

(And you think some of your friends are real let-downs.)

We can all learn a valuable lesson from Solomon. He was a truly wise man, and his wisdom was a gift from God. Sadly, he misused his gift. He made himself rich and powerful and surrounded himself with beautiful women, but he forgot to do one very important thing: humbly obey God.

Solomon wanted to do his own thing, live his own way. As a result, he endured lots of needless despair, despite having every material possession a man could possibly want.

Fortunately, this wise man finally wised up. Ecclesiastes is a rather depressing book, but it ends with some great advice for all of us:

> Now all has been heard; here is the conclusion of the matter: Fear God and keep his commandments, for this is the whole duty of man. For God will bring every deed into judgment, including every hidden thing, whether it is good or evil.
>
> —Ecclesiastes 12:13-14

Let me put into my words what I receive from this scripture:

The whole purpose of man's creation is that he reverence and worship God by obeying Him. All godly character must be rooted in obedience—it is the foundation of all happiness. No one can ever be truly happy without being obedient to God. Anything in our lives that is out of order will be brought into adjustment by obedience. Obedience is the whole duty of humanity.

Next time you're tempted to do things your own way, consider these words from Solomon. Obedience is each individual's responsibility before God.

Obedience becomes even more important when we realize that our choice to obey or disobey doesn't affect only us; it affects others, possibly many others. Think back to the Old Testament Israelites. Many of them died in the wilderness without ever reaching the Promised Land they sought for years and years. That's tragic. But what's more tragic is that many of these people's children died in the wilderness, too, as a result of their parents' disobedience.

The same kind of thing happens in your life. Your decisions affect other people—your family, your friends, your classmates, your teammates, and so on. And these effects can be positive or negative.

Recently, our oldest son came to me. "Mom," he said, "I have something to tell you, and I may cry, but hear me out. I have been thinking about you and Dad and the years you have put into this ministry, and all the times you chose to obey God and how it has not always been easy for you. I realize, Mom, that you and Dad have gone through things that nobody knows about, and I want you to know that this morning, God made me aware that I am benefiting greatly from your obedience, and I appreciate it."

What my son said meant a lot to me, and it reminded me of Romans 5:19: "For just as through the disobedience of the one man the many were made sinners, so also through the obedience of the one man the many will be made righteous."

Jesus provided the ultimate example of how one person's obedience can impact the lives of others. By being obedient even to the point of sacrificing His life on the cross, He saved the whole world.

You don't have to carry the weight of the whole world, but there are people in your life whom you can either lead out of the wilderness (of negativity, of rebellion, of apathy, or whatever) by your obedience or keep them wandering around as a result of your disobedience.

Obedience is a far-reaching thing. It can close the gates of hell and open the windows of heaven.

"Life is too hard for me to take—can't God make it easier?"

ere's a scenario that happens often in our ministry. A person comes to me for advice and prayer. I tell her what God's Word advises about the situation. She responds, "I hear what you're saying; God has been showing me the same thing. But, Joyce, what God wants me to do is just too hard!"

God has shown me that Satan often tries to inject this lie into people's minds, in an attempt to get them to give up. I used to believe this lie, but a few years ago, when God revealed this particular enemy tactic to me, He taught me to quit complaining about how hard everything seemed. He showed me that if I just kept obeying Him, things would get easier. He led me to Deuteronomy 30:11, which assures, "For this commandment which I command you this day is not too difficult for you, nor is it far off" (AMP).

We tend to make things harder than they need to be by whining our way through them. Negativity saps us of the energy and positive attitude we need to follow through on our goals. But God is beside us, telling us that His will is not too hard for us to follow—and that the realization of the hopes we have is not as far off as it sometimes seems to us.

True, God might lead you down a hard road, with difficult footing and muscle-busting inclines. But He'll be with you every step of the way, giving you the strength you need—the mental, physical, *and* spiritual strength.

"Life is so unfair—doesn't that give me the *right* to complain?"

studied these verses for years:

> For one is regarded favorably (is approved, acceptable, and
> thankworthy) if, as in the sight of God, he endures the pain
> of unjust suffering. [After all] what kind of glory [is there in
> it] if, when you do wrong and are punished for it, you take it
> patiently? But if you bear patiently with suffering [which

results] when you do right and that is undeserved, it is acceptable and pleasing to God.

—1 Peter 2:19-20

I tried to understand why in the world it pleased God so much to see me suffer. After all, doesn't the Bible say that Jesus bore my suffering and pain? If this was true, why was the suffering still happening to me?

Finally, I realized that suffering isn't even the focal point of the passage; it's the *attitude* one has about the suffering. If someone treats us wrongly, it pleases God if we handle it patiently. Think about those words carefully: God isn't pleased when we suffer; it's all about the attitude we adopt.

Jesus is our example in this. Peter tells us that Jesus was "reviled and insulted" and "abused." But He didn't revile or insult or abuse anyone in response. Instead, He entrusted every circumstance to God, His heavenly Father.

Jesus suffered courageously, gloriously. He didn't complain, even though every ounce of suffering He endured was unjust. He is our example of how to handle life when it is hard and unjust.

Something happened in our family a long time ago that illustrates the point. Our son, Daniel, returned from a mission trip to the Dominican Republic with a severe rash and several open sores on his arms. He, apparently, had a close encounter with the Dominican Republic's version of poison ivy.

Daniel's arms looked so bad that we knew we needed to get him to our family doctor. We called the doctor's office, only to find that our doctor was out that day. So, we made an appointment with his backup. Our daughter, Sandra, made the appointment. She explained that Daniel was a minor and that she would be bringing him in.

Sandra made the forty-five-minute drive to the doctor's office, only to be told by a nurse, "Oh, I'm sorry, but it is our policy not to treat minors unaccompanied by a parent."

Sandra explained that she had called earlier, specifically noting that she was bringing her brother in—as she had often done, due to her parents' work and travel schedules.

The nurse stood firm. No parent, no treatment.

Sandra could have really let the nurse have it. She had added this errand to an already jam-packed day. Her brother was hurting and needed help, and it looked like she would be driving ninety minutes round-trip, all for nothing. The whole endeavor seemed like a colossal, frustrating waste of time.

But Sandra remained calm and loving. She called her dad, who was visiting his mother at the time. He said that he would come over and take care of the situation. Earlier that day, he had felt led to stop by our offices to pick up some of my books and tapes, even though he had no idea what he was going to do with them.

He arrived at the medical office and the woman who helped him with Daniel's paperwork asked if he was a minister—and if he was Joyce Meyer's husband. He told her yes, and she said she had seen me on television. They talked awhile, and Dave ended up giving her one of my books on emotional healing, in response to a need he sensed in her. So, two people's needs were met that day: Daniel's physical ones and a medical professional's emotional ones.

Here's the main point of this story: What if Sandra had lost her patience with the nurse and started complaining and protesting? What kind of impression would she have left with the medical staff? Think about the woman at the registration desk. What if she had seen me on television, talking about developing a positive attitude, while one of my family members pitched a fit in public?

A lot of people in today's world are trying to find God, and what we *show* them is much more important than what we *tell* them. Sure, we need to talk about the Good News, but to talk, then negate what we say by bad behavior, is worse than never saying anything in the first place.

Sandra bore suffering and frustration with patience—exactly what God's Word calls for.

America: Whine Country?

Do you ever think the whole country is complaining? Have you noticed the long lines at various stores' customer-service departments and heard all of the grumbling that takes place when people finally get their turn at the front of the line?

There is so much grumbling and mumbling and murmuring today—and so little gratitude and appreciation. Do you hear your friends complaining about school, family, lack of money—and their "other" friends? Do you wonder if they complain about you, too, when you're not around?

I travel around the United States, and I want to tell you that there are people crammed into a homeless shelter right now, or standing in line at a soup kitchen, and they'd love to trade lives with these complainer friends of yours.

Have you heard one of your parents complain about "the boss," "the long work hours," or "the lousy pay"? I know dozens of poor people who would put up with the lousiest boss in the world just to have a job, any job.

Philippians 4:6 advises us, "Do not fret or have any anxiety about anything, but in every circumstance and in everything, by prayer and petition (definite requests), with thanksgiving, continue to make your wants known to God" (AMP).

In this scripture, the apostle Paul tells us how to face life's troubles: with thanksgiving in *every* circumstance. Notice how those words are carefully crafted. Paul isn't saying it's necessary to be thankful *for* every circumstance, but rather *in* every circumstance.

So, you don't have to pray, "God, thanks so much for this broken leg. I really love broken legs. I've always wanted one. Broken legs rule! Hey, could You break the other one, too?"

Instead, while you endure that broken leg and the healing process, you don't focus only on your leg. You keep your life in perspective and thank God for all the things that are going well in your life. You thank Him that your injuries aren't worse.

The Lord taught me this principle this way: "Joyce," He told me, "why should I give you the things you are asking for? You're not thankful for what you already have—you're filled with anxiety about them. Why should I give you something else to complain about?"

He showed me that if I couldn't offer prayer requests from a life foundation built on thankfulness, I would not get a favorable response. Neither will you. God does not say, "Pray with complaining." He says, "Pray with thanksgiving—every time."

Remember, true patience isn't just the ability to wait. Think back to those long customer-service lines. People there are waiting, but many of them are rolling their eyes, cursing under their breath, or heaving a heavy, exasperated sigh every twelve seconds. That's not patience.

Patience is the ability to keep a good attitude while you wait. That's what Jesus did.

"My behavior might be wrong—but it's not my fault."

Have you ever heard yourself saying any of the following?

"I don't usually lose my temper, but my mom knows how to push all of my buttons till I completely lose it!"

"My teacher hates me—that's why I'm always getting bad grades and getting into trouble in his class."

"Some of my friends are a bad influence on me; I never get into trouble unless I'm hanging around with them."

"I didn't want to be sexually active, but my boyfriend has some kind of power over me."

"I didn't want to try drugs, but my friends just wore me down."

When we do something wrong—and especially when we do something wrong and get caught—we are quick to point a finger in blame. Unfortunately, that finger is almost never pointed back at ourselves.

I know this from experience. Countless times in my own life, I pointed a finger at my husband, Dave.

I vividly remember praying to God, asking Him to change Dave. I had been studying my Bible, and as I read, I noted various flaws that were listed—and how Dave had a bunch of 'em. Dave needed to be different, I decided. And that would solve the problems in our relationship.

For example:

"If Dave didn't play golf on Saturdays, I wouldn't be so upset with him."

"If Dave would talk to me more, I wouldn't be so lonely."

"If Dave would buy me more presents, I wouldn't be so negative."

"If Dave helped me get out of the house more, I wouldn't be so bored."

Then the Lord spoke to me. "Joyce," He said, "Dave is not the problem . . . you are."

I responded maturely to this message. I cried and cried. I wept for three days straight, as God revealed to me just what it was like to live under the same roof with Joyce Meyer. He showed me how I tried to control everything, how I nagged and complained, how hard I was to please, and how negative I was. The list went on and on. The whole thing was a shock to my system, and a blow to my pride. But it was also the beginning of a God-sent recovery.

I had fallen into the habit of blaming every problem on something or someone other than myself. When I acted badly, I blamed Dave. Or I blamed my abuse. But God told me, "Joyce, abuse might be the *reason* you act this way, but don't let it become an *excuse* to stay this way!"

What a freeing life revelation that was: A reason doesn't have to be an excuse.

Satan, of course, wants us to keep using excuses. He wants to keep us from facing the truth. He tries to get us to cower in fear at the prospect of facing the truth about ourselves and our behavior. (Of course, we're more than capable of seeing the truth about others' problems, and we have no trouble telling them all about it.)

A key to being free from the Blame Game is to seek God's forgiveness. God is quick to forgive us if we truly repent, but we can't truly repent if we don't face the truth about our attitude and our mistakes. And facing the truth means going beyond just admitting we've done something wrong; it means not making excuses for that wrong behavior.

Here's an illustration: A neighbor called me one day and asked me to take her to the bank. Her car wouldn't start, and she needed to get to the bank right away, before it closed.

I was busy when she called, and I didn't want to be interrupted. So, I was rude and impatient with my neighbor. I hung up the phone—and realized immediately how terrible I had acted. I knew I needed to call her, apologize, and take her to the bank. But I found my mind filling up with excuses:

"I wasn't feeling good when she called."

"I was busy—she called at a really bad time for me."

"I was having a really rough day."

Deep in my spirit, though, I could sense God's Spirit telling me to quit making excuses. God revealed what I needed to do: "Just call her and tell her you were wrong, period. Say no more than, 'I was wrong, and there's no excuse for the way I behaved. Please forgive me and allow me to take you to the bank.'"

Saying those words was hard to do. My pride resisted. I wanted to run and hide from the responsibility, conjure up more excuses and not face the truth. But you can't hide from the truth, because the truth is light. It will find you in any dark corner you try to hide in.

But don't be stressed about facing the truth. The truth will set you free to live the abundant life God wants you to enjoy.

I understand that something in your past—or your present—may have hurt you. It might be a person, an event, or some kind of circumstance you've had to live with. These kinds of things can be the source of a wrong attitude and wrong behavior, but they don't have to become excuses.

I know without a doubt that many of my behavior problems were direct results of the many years of sexual, verbal, and emotional abuse I endured. And I was trapped in destructive behavior patterns as long as I excused them on the basis of being an abuse victim.

I'm here to tell you that you can definitely be free from your past, from everything that has brought you down. God promises, "I will never leave you nor forsake you," so hang onto Him and let Him lead you to freedom!

"I have a right to feel sorry for myself—my life stinks!"

A s I strived to leave the pain of my past behind and face the future with a positive mind-set, I found that self-pity was one of the hardest things to give up. I used pity for years, to comfort myself when I was hurting.

Then, during one of my "pity parties," the Lord spoke to me. "Joyce," He said, "you can be pitiful or powerful, but you cannot be both."

You see, the moment someone hurts us or we are stung by

disappointment, the enemy whispers lies to us, emphasizing how cruelly and unjustly we have been mistreated. We start to listen to the lies, and they wind themselves around us and make us prisoners of self-pity.

The Bible, however, doesn't give us permission to feel sorry for ourselves. In fact, one of the Bible's central messages is, "Focus on others, not yourself."

Recently, one of my speaking engagements was unexpectedly canceled. I had been looking forward to this event, and I began to feel deep disappointment setting in.

At one time in my life, a cancellation like this would have hurled me into a deep pit of self-pity. While down in the pit, I would have also criticized the organizers of the event, judging them and having all kinds of negative thoughts about them.

But I have learned that in this kind of situation, it's best to chill, to say nothing, rather than risk saying the wrong thing.

As I sat quietly, God began to show me the situation from the viewpoint of the people who had planned it. They had been unable to locate a building in which to hold the event, and God helped me realize how disappointing it must be to them to have their search fail. They were counting on the event—in fact, looking forward to it with great expectations, and now their hopes had been deflated.

I was amazed at how easy it was to avoid self-pity when I looked at the other people's side of things, rather than my own.

As Christians, we have a rare privilege when we experience disappointment; we can be "re-appointed," rather than disappointed. We can shift the focus off ourselves and onto someone else. God can give us a new beginning—if we don't allow self-pity to keep us trapped in old patterns.

I wasted so many years of my life feeling sorry for myself. I became addicted to self-pity. It became like an automatic response to certain stimuli in my life. For me, when disappointment came, I responded with self-pity.

Instead of "thinking about what I was thinking about," I let wrong thoughts fill up my mind. And the more wrong thoughts that piled up, the more pitiful I felt.

I often tell stories about the early years of my marriage. During football season, Dave spent every Sunday afternoon watching NFL games on TV. (And if it wasn't football season, it was some other "ball" season.) Dave enjoyed sports year-round. He liked anything that involved a bouncing ball and could easily get caught up in a game. So caught up that he didn't even know I existed. As you might guess, I didn't enjoy *any* sport.

One day, I stood in front of Dave and said, "I don't feel well at all; I feel like I'm going to die."

Without even raising his eyes from the screen, he replied, "Uh-huh, that's nice, dear."

So, I spent many Sunday afternoons angry and in self-pity. I would get mad at Dave and start cleaning the house. I was trying to make him feel guilty for sitting there and enjoying himself while I was being miserable. I would storm around the house, like a cleaning tornado. I slammed doors and drawers, marched back and forth through the room where he sat, pushing the vacuum cleaner, making a loud display of how hard I was working.

I was trying to get his attention, but he hardly noticed me. So, I would give up, go to the back of the house, sit on the bathroom floor, and cry. The more I cried, the more pitiful I felt. (In later years, God revealed to me why women go to the bathroom to cry: It's because most bathrooms have large mirrors, into which we can stare and see how truly pitiful we look.)

After long fits of crying, I looked so bad that seeing my reflection made me start crying all over again. Then, finally, I would make one last sorrowful trip through the family room, trudging slowly and pitifully. Occasionally, Dave would look up long enough to see me—and ask me if I was on my way to the kitchen and if I would bring him some iced tea.

The bottom line: The pity-approach didn't work. Instead, I exhausted myself emotionally, often making myself physically sick, as well.

In time, I learned that God won't deliver you by your own hand, but by His. Only God can change people. Believe me, nobody but the Almighty Himself could have discouraged Dave from watching so much sports on TV.

As I learned to trust the Lord with this matter—and quit wallowing in self-pity when I didn't get my way—I saw Dave come into balance about his sports-watching.

Dave still enjoys sports, but that fact doesn't bother me anymore. I just use his TV time to do things I really enjoy—instead of furious housecleaning.

If I truly need or want Dave to spend a Sunday afternoon with me, I sweetly—not angrily—ask him. Most of the time, he willingly alters his plans.

Sure, there are still times when I don't get my way. But as soon as I feel my emotions starting to rise, I pray, "Oh, God, help me pass this test." And He is faithful to help me pass the test—with flying colors.

"I'm not a very good person, so I don't deserve God's blessings."

We've talked about blaming others for the bad things in our lives, and a lot of people do that. But there's a flip-side to the blame game. Some people blame themselves for everything bad in their lives. I'm not talking about the healthy habit of taking responsibility for your actions and reactions; I'm talking about feeling unworthy, so unworthy that you think you deserve every lousy thing that happens to you.

Sadly, many people endure double doses of blame. For example, a teen girl might hate her uncle for the way he physically abused her, but at the same time, she might think that there is something wrong, something impure about her or she wouldn't have been a target for the abuse in the first place.

I used to think this way. I criticized and judged and blamed other people, but I also had a shame-based nature. I often blamed myself for the bad things that happened to me—even though a lot of it happened in my childhood and there was nothing I could have done to stop it. I felt disgraced.

Grace is God's favor, God's power, given to us as a free gift. Grace helps us do with ease things we couldn't do on our own. *Disgrace*, on the other hand, comes from Satan, not the Lord. Disgrace tells us, "You're no good. You should be ashamed of yourself for what you've done, for the way you think. You're not worthy of God's love or help."

Disgrace poisons your mind. You feel ashamed of what has been done to you, but you also feel ashamed of yourself, as a person. This was how I felt. Deep down inside, I simply did not like who I was.

The beauty of God's forgiveness is that it allows us to respond to negative thoughts like: "You don't deserve God's blessings!" with "I know I don't, but I can have them anyway!"

Here's the truth: Nobody deserves God's blessings. If they could be earned, they wouldn't be blessings. The book of Romans talks about the wages of sin being death, but the free gift of God being eternal life. Note the distinction between what we can earn and what God gives to us out of His sheer grace and love.

We aren't worthy of God's blessings. But we can humbly and gratefully accept them. We can enjoy God's blessings and have our socks rocked by how good He is and how much He loves us!

"Why shouldn't I be jealous? Most of the people I know are better off than I am!"

ccording to the world's system, the winner takes all. If you can't be number one, you're a loser. The message we get so often today is, "Get to the top, no matter who you have to hurt on the way up."

The Bible, conversely, teaches us that there is no such thing as real peace until we are free from the need to be richer, stronger, more popular, better-looking, and more successful than everybody else.

Have you ever seen the various "reality shows" and how even a made-for-TV competition can turn complete strangers into bitter enemies? The competition gets so out-of-balance that the participants forget that they are all getting the privilege of being on national television, with all its perks. Instead of enjoying an opportunity that few people will ever receive, they end up arguing with each other, backstabbing each other, and making each other—and themselves—miserable.

Sure, you should do your best at school, in sports, in music or drama, or whatever your thing is. The problem comes when you can't enjoy what you're doing unless you win—unless you get first chair, first place, or first prize. If you become jealous or bitter every time you see someone who has something you don't, your life is going to be miserable.

I'll go so far as to say that jealousy and envy are torments straight from hell. I spent many years envying anyone who looked better than I did, or had talents I didn't have. I secretly lived in competition with others who had ministries like mine. It was so important to me that "my" ministry be bigger in size and scope, attract more attendees to events, and boast a bigger budget than anyone else's. If some other person's ministry surpassed mine in any way, I wanted to be happy for that person—because God was blessing him or her—but something inside me would just not allow me to feel the way I should.

I remember when a friend of mine once received a gift from the Lord—a gift that I had wanted a long time. I didn't consider this friend to be as "spiritual" as I, so I became very jealous when she showed up at my front door, bubbling with the news of what God had done for her. I pretended to be happy, but in my heart I wasn't.

After my friend left, I was shocked at the thoughts parading through my mind. I resented God for blessing this woman, because I didn't think she deserved it. After all, I had stayed home, fasting and praying, while she ran around with her friends, having a good time. I was a religious snob.

God, however, had other plans. He knew what I really needed, while I was focused on what I *wanted*. He knew that I needed to get rid of my bad attitude much more than I needed the "blessing" for which I was praying and believing Him. God arranged the circumstances so that I could face myself and expose what the enemy was doing to my attitude.

Fortunately, as I better understood who I was in Jesus' eyes, I was freed from the need to compare "mine" with "theirs." The more I learned to trust God, the more freedom I enjoyed. I learned that my heavenly Father loves me and will do whatever is best for me.

What God does for me and what He does for you might not be the same as what He does for someone else. But remember Jesus' advice to His disciple Peter. Jesus was telling Peter about some of the hardships he would have to endure in order to serve and glorify his Lord. Peter turned to his fellow disciple John and said, "What about him?" (Peter wanted to make sure that if he was destined to suffer, John would be right beside him, enduring those hard times, too.)

Jesus politely told Peter to mind his own business. He instructed Peter, "Don't be concerned about what I choose to do with someone else—you follow Me!"

You'll find something amazing as you choose to follow your Lord: He wants to bless you far beyond your desire to be blessed! But He also loves you so much that He won't bless you beyond your capacity to handle the blessings properly and to give Him the glory for the success you enjoy.

Back when I was jealous of my friend, God already had a plan for my ministry. He intended to make me steward over a ministry that would reach millions of people via TV, radio, books, seminars, and more. But He wasn't going to bring these plans to fruition until I "grew up" in Him.

Take stock of your jealous thoughts and feelings. Don't be afraid to be honest with yourself—and with God. He knows how you feel anyway, so you might as well talk with Him about it.

Then, when you recognize jealousy setting up outposts in your mind, have a little talk with yourself. Say, *What good will it do me to be jealous of a friend or classmate? God isn't going to bless me for being jealous; that's not the way He works. God has a plan for my life, and I'm going to trust Him to do what is best for me. It isn't any of my business what He chooses to do for other people.*

When you're done with this self-talk, try praying that those "fortunate" people you know will be blessed even more. Seriously. It's good for you.

I say prayers like this: "God, I pray for _____ to be blessed even more than she is now. Cause her to prosper; bless her in every way. I am praying this by faith, because I admit I feel jealous of her, inferior to her, but I choose to do this Your way, whether I feel like it or not."

In the big picture, what's the use of all the struggling to get ahead of someone else? As soon as we become number one, someone will be trying to topple us from our pedestal.

Think of sports. World and Olympic records are broken all the time. Teams that were championship contenders a few years ago languish at the bottoms of their divisions today.

God has helped me understand that "shooting stars" flash across the sky and earn lots of attention, but they're not around for long. He told me that it is much better to be around for the long haul, to hang in there and do what He's asked me to do, to the best of my ability. He, not I, is in charge of my reputation. Whatever God asks me to do is all right with me. Why? Because He knows what I can handle way better than I do.

Set your mind to be happy for others and trust God with your life. Tear down the walls of jealousy that imprison your mind and limit your happiness. Leave the possibilities to God. He will amaze you.

WWJT Is Your WMD!

But we have the mind of Christ (the Messiah) and do
hold the thoughts (feelings and purposes) of His heart.
—1 Corinthians 2:16 (AMP)

You've probably seen people sporting WWJD bracelets or T-shirts. Maybe you even wear one yourself. WWJD is a great concept. It helps people ask, "What would Jesus do?" before taking action.

However, I think WWJD is only half the battle. I want to introduce you to a new four-letter combo: WWJT. It stands for *What Would Jesus Think?* In other words, *which* things would Jesus spend time thinking about, and *how* would He think about them?

It is important to arm yourself with WWJT as your WMD—your Weapon of Mass Destruction—to shoot down the attacks of the enemy on your mind. You need to think like Jesus if you want to act like Jesus. Now, you might be saying, "That's impossible, Joyce. Jesus was perfect and all-wise. I might be able to *improve* the way I think, but I'll never be able to think the way He did!"

You think you can't think like Jesus? Think again! You can do this. When God adopts you into His family, He gives you a new spirit, a new heart, and the ability to renew your mind so that you think as Jesus does.

Here's a look at this concept in action. Imagine that one of your friends backstabs you—breaks a confidence or says something untrue and hurtful about you. Your "natural" reaction might be to get angry, maybe even start hating your friend and plotting revenge. The results? Stress, tension, headaches, a sick feeling in your gut, fatigue, and sleeplessness, just to name a few. The natural mind-set can suck the life out of you.

On the other hand, as your mind is renewed and you begin to adopt the WWJT concept, your response is different. Rather than focusing only on the injustice, you see things in perspective. You realize that God has blessed you and been good to you in dozens of different ways. So you don't let one incident overshadow everything else. In addition, you think of Jesus' loving, forgiving attitude, even toward His enemies. Maybe you go to your friend and try to find out what sparked the unfortunate behavior. You try to clear things up. And you don't repay evil with more evil.

When you adopt the mind of Christ, you fill yourself up with life, rather than let it get drained out of you.

Does thinking the way Jesus thought—and behaving the way He behaved—really work? Even in tough areas, like sexual purity? After all, many people who make "purity pledges" end up becoming sexually active.

Here is a real-life interview with a young woman who resolved to stay pure until marriage—and honored that commitment. Read what she has to say, and you be the judge.

Your friends who became sexually active as teens—are any of them with their partners from those years?

No. You change so much after your teen years. That's why I encourage teens I talk with to stay strong. When you are a teen, you're still finding out who you are. You don't know what you'll be like in a few years, and you don't know what your current boyfriend or girlfriend will be like. I know that, for me, my idea of the kind of guy I wanted to spend my life with changed dramatically once I left my teen years behind.

How do your friends who didn't stay pure sexually feel about it now?

So many of my friends have expressed regret to me. They feel guilty. And they feel bad about their spouses' sexual past, as well. One of my friends held to the standard, but her husband didn't. He didn't tell her about his past until after they were engaged. She felt so bad that she wouldn't be able to be her husband's "first." She had all these insecurities—about disease, about her husband comparing her to his previous partners—that kind of thing.

As a young married person, how do you feel today about your commitment to purity?

It's worth it to stay a virgin until you are married. It's more than worth it. I knew God would reward me for obeying Him, but the reward was greater than I ever imagined. I'm not saying that people who make a mistake can't find grace and forgiveness and have a fulfilling marriage, but it makes it so much sweeter if you wait. I am thankful that my husband and I didn't drag any sexual baggage into our relationship. It made things more intimate. The Bible talks about a man and a woman becoming "one flesh," a oneness that is emotional, physical, and spiritual. Think about it—how can you become "one" with a bunch of different people?

Now, how do we go about thinking like Jesus? Try these suggestions . . .

1. **Think positive thoughts.** Can you imagine Jesus walking around with a head full of negative thoughts? Could He have spoken so many uplifting, inspiring messages if His mind was clouded with negativity?

   Jesus was and is pure positivity, and if you and I want to walk with Him, we have to walk to a positive beat. I am not talking about forcing fake positivity into your head; I'm talking about having an outlook that doesn't forget about the good things when hard times hit, an outlook that expects the best, rather than dreading the worst.

   Think about Jesus. He was lied about, deserted, ridiculed, misunderstood, betrayed, and much worse. Yet in the midst of all the negative, He remained positive. He could always find uplifting, encouraging words to say. He always gave hope to those who approached Him.

The mind of Christ is a positive mind. Therefore, any time we get negative, we aren't operating with the mind of Christ. Millions of people today suffer from depression, and I don't believe it's possible to be depressed without being negative, too. (I do understand that sometimes the cause of depression is medical/chemical, but even in these cases, negativity will only make depression and its symptoms worse.)

God does not want you to be negative. Psalm 3:3 says that God is our glory and "the lifter of our heads." He wants you to approach life with your head held high.

The devil, meanwhile, wants to beat you down. And nothing will beat you down more than a negative mind. Life's problems can threaten to make you discouraged, but being negative won't solve a single problem. It will only make every problem worse. Positive thoughts, on the other hand, will bring light to the dark places in your life.

2. **Resist the negativity and despair that rob you of life.** Our spirits, empowered and encouraged by God's Spirit, are powerful and free. Satan seeks to put a leash on our spirits and beat them down by filling us with darkness and gloom. It is vital, then, to resist the feelings of despair and depression *immediately* upon sensing their arrival. The longer you allow despair to nibble at you, the harder it becomes to resist. Think of despair like a tick. You want to flick it off before it buries its head in your skin.

3. **Remember the good times.** In Psalm 143:5, the psalmist wrote, "I remember the days of old; I meditate on all Your doings; I ponder the work of Your hands" (AMP).

When hard times hit us and knock us backward, it's easy to forget all the progress we have made. Don't let this happen to you. Don't forget all the battles you have won, with God at your side. Take stock of all the territory you have conquered. Don't abandon it in the face of one setback. You wouldn't kick LeBron James off your basketball team for one missed dunk, forgetting all the dunks he had thrown down before.

Remember all that God has done for you—and for others, too. The God who brought you to this point in your life is fully capable of guiding your present and future. And as you follow Him, you'll pile up even more good memories to sustain you during the next challenging season of your life.

4. **Seek the Lord through prayer and praise.** If you follow the Bible's accounts of Jesus' life, one thing becomes clear. Jesus was devoted to prayer. He prayed to God and thanked Him publicly, and He often withdrew from those around Him to spend time in solitary prayer with His heavenly Father. It's important to note that Jesus didn't spend all of His time preaching, teaching, healing, and feeding people. If prayer time was important to Jesus, that's a powerful example for us.

God alone can water your thirsty soul. Don't be fooled into thinking that anything else can satisfy you completely. God is eager to hear from you. He wants to meet your needs, and He wants you to spend time with Him.

Prayer time, of course, isn't just a time for you to talk to God. It's a time to listen to Him, as well. Jesus sought His Father's guidance, reflecting the attitude of the psalmist in Psalm 143:8: "Cause me to hear your loving-kindness in the morning, for on You do I lean and in You do I trust. Cause me to know the way wherein I should walk, for I lift up my inner self to You" (AMP).

In your prayer time, allow God to assure you of His lovingkindness; be attentive to His attention and direction.

Remember, a Christ-like mind is a prayerful mind.

5. **Meditate on God and His works.** You don't have to be in a church to think about God and marvel at His wonders. I enjoy watching TV shows about nature, animals, ocean life, etc., because they portray God's awesome power and boundless creativity. They remind me how God is the sustainer of all life.

One of my favorite verses is Psalm 17:15, which says of the Lord, "I shall be fully satisfied, when I awake [to find myself] beholding Your form [and having sweet communion with You]" (AMP).

I spent many unhappy days because I used to start thinking about all the wrong things the moment I awoke each morning. I can truly say that I have been fully satisfied since the Holy Spirit has helped me begin each day with the mind of Christ. Fellowshipping with God early in the morning is one sure way to begin enjoying the life that each day brings.

6. **Operate from a base of love.** When you're following the previous suggestion, make sure you devote some of your God-meditation time to His pure love. The Bible goes so far as to say "God is love" (1 John 4:8), but it's hard to experience God's love without meditating on it.

I remember when I began my ministry. Before the first meeting I conducted, I asked the Lord what He wanted me to teach. He responded, "Tell My people that I love them."

"They know that," I replied. "I want to teach them something really powerful, not a Sunday-school lesson out of John 3:16."

Then the Lord said to me, "Very few of My people really

know how much I love them. If they did, they would act differently."

So, I began to study the subject of receiving God's love. And I realized that I was in desperate need of it myself. The Lord led me to 1 John 4:16, which states that we should be conscious—actively aware of—God's love.

Now, I had a vague sort of understanding that God loved me, but God's love is meant to be a powerful force in our lives, just as it was in Jesus' life. As Jesus demonstrated, love can take us through even the most painful, humiliating trials and stand on the other side, victorious.

I studied the subject of God's love for a long time, and as I did, I became increasingly conscious and aware of God's love for me. I thought about that love. I proclaimed it out loud. I learned scriptures about God's love and meditated on them, recited them aloud. I did this over and over for months, and the amazing revelation of God's love became more and more of a reality to me.

Today, God's love is so real to me that even in hard times I am comforted by the "conscious knowing" that He loves me and that I no longer have to live in fear. I wish the same knowledge for you.

Let love be your base camp in the battle for your mind. Let it be a driving, energizing force for you.

7. **Be righteousness-conscious, not sin-conscious.** Many people are tormented by negative thoughts about themselves. They think God must be displeased with them because of all their weaknesses and failures.

How much time have you wasted living in a state of guilt and condemnation? Note that I referred to time "wasted," not

time merely "spent." That's because time spent thinking negatively is absolutely wasted. No matter the terrible state you are
in when you come to God, He can make you pure and clean.
He will forgive all of your sins. Second Corinthians 5:21 says
that through Christ, we become the righteousness of God
Himself. Ponder that concept for a moment.

Christ enables you to be made into righteousness. You are
right before God. So is everyone else who turns to Him. Let
this knowledge drive how you think about yourself and others.
Encourage yourself. Encourage those around you.

8. **Be thankful.** Jesus was a living example of Psalm 34:1, in
which David proclaims, "I will extol the LORD at all times; his
praise will always be on my lips." He thanked God during
tragic times, during triumphant times, even at mealtimes.

We can emulate Jesus' mind-set and lifestyle by being grateful
people, people filled with gratitude not only toward God but also
toward those around us. When someone does something nice for
you, let him or her know that you appreciate it. Show appreciation to your family. Sure, they have faults, but don't take for
granted the way they have blessed your life.

I have been married a long time, and my husband knows I appreciate him. But I still *tell* him how much I appreciate him. I
thank him for being such a very patient man. I tell him about his
many other really good qualities. When we let people know we
appreciate them, we build and maintain strong relationships with
them.

I deal with a lot of people, and it continues to amaze me how
some people are extremely thankful for every small blessing,
while others are never satisfied, no matter how much is done for

them. They think they deserve every good thing they get, so they seldom express appreciation.

Expressing appreciation is important. It's good for people to hear, and it releases joy in us as we share it.

So, meditate daily on all the things you have to be thankful for. Tell God, "Thank You!" As you do, you will find your heart filling up with life and light.

If you believe God, you have the mind of Christ. I can't think of much better news to share with you than that. I hope the ideas in this concluding chapter will help you use that mind of Christ—to ask yourself continually, "WWJT?" Which things would Jesus think about? (Remember, if He wouldn't think about something, you shouldn't, either.) And *how* would He think about the things that are worth pondering?

By keeping continual watch over your thoughts, you can ensure that no damaging enemy thoughts creep into your mind.

Satan has launched a war against your mind, but you have the weapons to win—weapons like love, like prayer. And your arsenal includes the ability to think as Jesus did, to have the mind of Christ. Think about the implication of those last two sentences: Does Satan have a chance if he's not merely battling your mind, but Christ's, as well? He's gonna get smoked.

With that truth in mind, it's my heartfelt prayer that this book will help you blast away at every lie, imagination, or theory that stands against God. And I pray that your every thought will be guided by our Lord Jesus Christ, who loves you with an everlasting love.

NOTES

CHAPTER 1

1. *Christian Retailing*, August 22, 2005, p. 48.
2. "Does Watching Sex on Television Influence Teens' Sexual Activity?" www.rand.org/publications/RB/RB9068/RB9068.pdf. Accessed 11/22/05.
3. Richards, Sarah E. "She Drank Herself to Death," *Seventeen Magazine*, May 2005, pp. 112–13. www.samspadyfoundation.org/newsletter/405.pdf. Accessed 11/22/05.
4. Staff writer, "Racism Today," *Seventeen Magazine*, May 2005, pp. 114–15.
5. "Parents and Teen Pregnancy: What Surveys Show," http://www.teenpregnancy .org/resources/data/parentpoll2004.asp. Accessed 11/22/05.
6. "Fact Sheet: Sobering Facts on Teens and Alcohol," http://www.teenpregnancy .org/resources/reading/fact_sheets/alcohol.asp. Accessed 11/22/05.
7. Everson, Eva Marie and Jessica. *Sex, Lies, and the Media* (Colorado Springs: Cook Communications, 2005).
8. "NAHIC 2004 Fact Sheet on Suicide," http://nahic.ucsf.edu/downloads/ Suicide.pdf. Accessed 11/22/05.
9. "Research & Data: Stats and Facts," www.purerevolution.com/purerevolution/ adult/. Accessed 10/28/05.
10. Todd and Jedd Hafer, *Wake Up and Smell the Pizza* (Minneapolis, MN: Bethany House Publishers, 2005).
11. Springen, Karen, "Beyond the Birds and the Bees," *Newsweek*, April 25, 2005, p. 61.
12. "Partnership for a Drug-Free America," as reported in *Runner's World*, October 2005.

13. Eva Marie and Jessica Everson, *Sex, Lies, and the Media* (Colorado Springs: Cook Communications, 2005). (Also, the Kaiser Family Foundation Web site, kff.org, reports that 18 percent of all 9–12th-grade males have had four or more sexual partners.)

CHAPTER 6

1. www.samspadyfoundation.org/newsletter/405.pdf. Accessed 11/22/05.
2. "White Paper: Adolescent Sexuality," www.plannedparenthood.org/pp2/portal/files/portal/medicalinfo/teensexualhealth/white-adolescent-sexuality-01.xml. Accessed 11/22/05.
3. "Does Watching Sex on Television Influence Teens' Sexual Activity?" www.rand.org/publications/RB/RB9068/RB9068.pdf. Accessed 11/22/05.
4. "MMWR: Youth Risk Behavior Surveillance—United States, 2003: Sexual Intercourse Before Age 13 Years," http://www.cdc.gov/mmwr/PDF/SS/SS5302.pdf, p. 20, Accessed 11/22/05.
5. "Making the Case for Financial Literacy: Undergraduate and Graduate Students," www.jumpstartcoalition.com/upload/Personal%20Financial%20Stats%202005%20Letterhead.doc. Accessed 11/22/05.
6. Staff writer, "Playing Risk," *Men's Health*, January/February 2005, p. 36.
7. Ibid.
8. Ibid.
9. "Marijuana & Mental Health: An Open Letter to Parents," www.theantidrug.com/drug_info/mjmh_open_letter.asp. Accessed 10/28/05.
10. Broadman-Grimm, M. D., Karen. "Sex Q & A," *Seventeen*, May 2005, p. 83.
11. Ibid.
12. Grumman, Rachel. "Sex Ed.," *Seventeen*, October 2005, p. 102.
13. "Teenage drinking key findings," www.ama-assn.org/ama1/pub/upload/mm/388/keyfindings.pdf. Accessed 11/22/05.

CHAPTER 8

1. "Generation Perfect," *Seventeen*, October 2005, pp. 149–50.

PART 3: INTRODUCTION

1. "The Chart: Top Ten List," *Rolling Stone*, April 7, 2005, p. 32.
2. Ibid.

CHAPTER 11

1. W. E. Vine, *An Expository Dictionary of New Testament Words* (Old Tappan, NJ: Fleming H. Revell, 1940).

BIBLIOGRAPHY

Everson, Eva Marie and Jessica. *Sex, Lies, and the Media*. Colorado Springs: Cook Communications, 2005.

Hafer, Todd and Jedd. *Wake Up and Smell the Pizza*. Minneapolis, MN: Bethany House Publishers, 2005.

Random House Unabridged Dictionary, 2nd ed. New York: Random House, 1993.

Strong, James. *The New Strong's Exhaustive Concordance of the Bible*. Nashville: Thomas Nelson Publishers, 1984.

Vine, W. E. *An Expository Dictionary of New Testament Words*. Old Tappan: Fleming H. Revell Company, 1940.

Webster's II Riverside University Dictionary. Boston: Houghton Mifflin Company, 1984.

ABOUT THE AUTHOR

JOYCE MEYER, one of the world's leading practical Bible teachers, has been teaching the Word of God since 1976 and has been in full-time ministry since 1980. A #1 *New York Times* bestselling author, she has written nearly ninety inspirational books, including *Power Thoughts, 100 Ways to Simplify Your Life*, the entire Battlefield of the Mind family of books, her first venture into fiction with *The Penny*, and many others. She has also released thousands of audio teachings, as well as a complete video library. Joyce's *Enjoying Everyday Life* radio and television programs are broadcast around the world, and she travels extensively conducting conferences. Joyce and her husband, Dave, are the parents of four grown children and make their home in St. Louis, Missouri.

TO CONTACT THE AUTHOR, PLEASE WRITE:

Joyce Meyer Ministries
P.O. Box 655
Fenton, MO 63026
USA
(636) 349-0303
www.joycemeyer.org

Joyce Meyer Ministries—Canada
P.O. Box 7700
Vancouver, BC V6B 4E2
Canada
(800) 868-1002

Joyce Meyer Ministries—Australia
Locked Bag 77
Mansfield Delivery Centre
Queensland 4122
Australia
(07) 3349 1200

Joyce Meyer Ministries—England
P.O. Box 1549
Windsor SL4 1GT
United Kingdom
01753 831102

Joyce Meyer Ministries—South Africa
P.O. Box 5
Cape Town 8000
South Africa
(27) 21-701-1056

OTHER BOOKS BY JOYCE MEYER

100 Ways to Simplify Your Life

21 Ways to Finding Peace and Happiness

Any Minute

Approval Addiction

The Battle Belongs to the Lord

Battlefield of the Mind *

Battlefield of the Mind Devotional

Be Anxious for Nothing *

Be Healed in Jesus' Name

Beauty for Ashes (Revised Edition)

Being the Person God Made You to Be

Celebration of Simplicity

The Confident Woman Devotional

Do It Afraid!

Do Yourself a Favor...Forgive

Don't Dread

Eat the Cookie...Buy the Shoes

Eight Ways to Keep the Devil Under Your Feet

Ending Your Day Right

*Enjoying Where You Are on the Way to
Where You Are Going*

The Everyday Life Bible

* Study guide available for this title

Check out the entire
BATTLEFIELD of the MIND
family of books!

Battlefield of the Mind

If you suffer from negative
thoughts, Joyce Meyer can help.
With her million-copy bestseller,
Joyce Meyer shows how you
can change your life by simply
changing your mind. Gain control over your mind, learn to be
patient, and conquer the damaging thoughts that influence your
life every day.

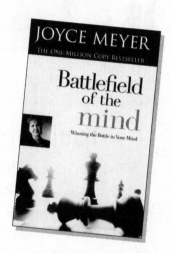

and more . . .

Battlefield of the Mind
Study Guide

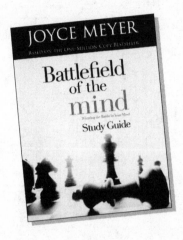

The thought-provoking questions in this companion study guide will help you search for truths that you can apply to your life immediately. Ideal for both individual and group use, the workbook format provides space to fill in answers to each question, and you can check your work with the special answer section in the back.

Battlefield of the Mind
Devotional

This devotional offers short, powerful messages you can read from day to day. The readings will help you to identify the distorted thinking of the enemy, effectively confront them and find victory in transforming your thinking. Each reading offers you strength, encouragement and most importantly, triumph in the battlefield!

Battlefield of the Mind
for Teens

Joyce Meyer partners with popular author and speaker Todd Hafer to bring her respected wisdom and sound advice to today's teens— a group that desperately needs to hear Joyce's message. Using contemporary language, well-timed humor, powerful statistics, and teen-appropriate applications and calls to action, this book offers teens a relevant and engaging version of the bestselling original.

Battlefield of the Mind
for Kids

Partnering with Karen Moore, Joyce Meyer provides the same inspiring message of encouragement and hope as the original edition for adults, but in a manner specifically geared for children. Written in an up-beat style and filled with interesting stories, this book will appeal to these readers at a time when they need it most—their preteen years.